# SOUTHAMPTON

## GATEWAY TO THE WORLD

# SOUTHAMPTON
## GATEWAY TO THE WORLD

ALASTAIR ARNOTT

First published 2010

The History Press
The Mill, Brimscombe Port
Stroud, Gloucestershire, GL5 2QG
www.thehistorypress.co.uk

British Library Cataloguing in Publication Data.
A catalogue record for this book is available from the British Library.

ISBN 978 0 7524 5357 6

Typesetting and origination by The History Press
Printed in Great Britain

# CONTENTS

# FOREWORD

Southampton owes its existence to its position in the estuary of the River Solent on the South Coast of England, sheltered from the storms that can rage along the Channel and with access, via the tributaries of the Test and Itchen, to the rich and productive settlements inland.

From its earliest days the town, and later the city, looked outward. English wool, the finest in the world, was sent from here across the Channel in exchange for wine, olive oil and other luxury goods. As generation succeeded generation the settlement continued to develop, both as a trading post and also as a technologically innovative and outward-looking port where seafarers from every nation were made welcome.

Southampton was not, of course, alone in its ability to develop and expand. Galleys from the Mediterranean were replaced with sailing ships which were in turn supplanted by steamers and later by the diesel-powered leviathans that carry containers around the globe. Each change necessitated an alteration to the infrastructure of the port and an increase in the number of services required to keep the different types of vessel seaworthy and safe.

The twentieth century saw another major change in the development of passenger and cruise ships as increasing numbers of intelligent, interested people eschewed the printed travel guides and the television and took advantage of the facilities offered to see the world for themselves. Southampton is now the UK's major cruising port and assists many thousands of passengers to achieve their dreams of overseas travel in a comfort and style that our ancestors could never have dreamed of.

All of these changes have left their mark upon the town, but particularly at the point where the land meets the sea. Generations of local people have worked here, as porters and shipwrights, pilots, stevedores and a thousand and one other occupations, each with a particular part to play and occupying a particular place. The daily lives of these men and women are essential to the success of the city, and the port employees are fondly spoken of in terms of a hard-working family dedicated to the continual flow of international trade.

Over the years the port itself has changed, with the building of quaysides and later of docks; the introduction of cranes and other mechanical means of loading and unloading cargo; and most recently the terminals in which cruise passengers can be made welcome. This book is a chronicle of those changes and developments that together have ensured that Southampton remains the hub of international commerce and passenger traffic – that it is still the 'Gateway to the World'.

# INTRODUCTION

Over a period of many years, the author has been asked by numerous individuals to iden-
tify and date various features making up the waterfront of Southampton in order that the
content of photographs and paintings could be explained. One of the motives behind
the creation of this book is to assist in the understanding of that ever-changing scene.
Such a work could never be fully comprehensive as the primary sources of information,
especially for the later period, have almost exclusively been those produced by the various owners and operators of the dock facilities and this may lead to bias. It does, however,
give a fresh perspective on life in a major port.

The idea has been to chronicle events without intending to be judgemental about
their impact or appropriateness. Shipbuilding, until the closure of Vosper Thornycroft
in 2003, has been a major industry in Southampton for many years, although it is not
chronicled in much detail here. For this, and some idea of the ancillary industries supporting shipping, the reader should consult *Maritime Southampton* by the author. Many of
the illustrations complement the story of the port as related here.

The sculpture commissioned by the Southern Railway to mark the centenary of the
Docks was essentially a globe of the world and this device had also featured on the
weather vane of the Harbour Board offices more than a decade earlier. Globes were also
embodied in the decoration of the original Ocean Terminal, surmounting the obelisk in
the tourist class waiting room and in the weather vane outside. One of the earliest advertisements relating to the Docks, produced in 1924 by the Southern Railway, carried the
slogan, 'Southampton Docks Link the World'. By 1930 another railway publication, the
souvenir guidebook given to visitors, used both the phrases 'the Gateway of the World'
and 'Gateway to the World' in its text. Which applies no doubt depends on one's direction
of travel.

The title has, however, been modified to suit the occasion. In 1938 it became 'Gateway
to the Empire' for the Empire Exhibition, and this has been revived as part of the titles of
books, most recently in 2007. One may not be able to go directly to all the places from
Accra to Zanzibar as the alphabet of destinations once recorded, although Southampton
has recently been described as the 'Cruise Capital of Northern Europe'. Later attempts at
a summary of the virtues of Southampton produced 'The Great Distributing Port of the
World's Commerce' in 1932 and 'Britain's Most Progressive Port' in 1936.

However, in 1936 Leslie Carr produced one of his famous posters for the Southern Railway, for which he chose the title 'Gateway to the World'. It seems to be the most evocative and accurate description of the function of the Port of Southampton and has stuck ever since. This book is the story of how the port rose to achieve its gateway status.

*Note*

In most cases where measurements have been taken from sources using Imperial units, the modern S.I. measure has been provided in brackets alongside the original, viz. 40 gallons (180 litres), or 20 acres (8 hectares).

This has not been done with tons/tonnes. As some readers will know, a ton is 2,240 pounds (lb). Now 1,000kg is equivalent to 2,200lb and is known as a metric ton or tonne. It is 98.2 per cent of an Imperial ton and the difference for the purpose of this book is negligible. The original figures have therefore been quoted unaltered.

# ACKNOWLEDGEMENTS

The author would like to thank the following individuals and organisations for their invaluable assistance, without which this book would not have been completed. A number of individuals have permitted access to their private collections but have asked to remain anonymous.

Particular thanks are owed to Bert Moody, Stan Roberts and Maureen Webber, without whose contributions this book would be infinitely the poorer. Other individuals who have generously contributed their time and expertise are: Ian Abrahams; Jim Brown; Nigel Burt; Lindsay Ford; Ron Hancock; John Horne; Giles Hudson; Roger Jenkins; Kevin Lockyer; Doug Morrison; and Lorraine Nottley.

My grateful thanks are also owed to: Associated British Ports; Bitterne Local History Society; Carnival UK; DP World Southampton; ExxonMobil Fawley; Glasgow University; C.G. Hibbert & Co. Ltd; Institution of Civil Engineers; National Oceanography Centre; Southampton University; Royal Gloucester Lodge; Science Museum; Southampton City Council Arts and Heritage Services; Unilever Archives.

# 1

# A SAFE ANCHORAGE

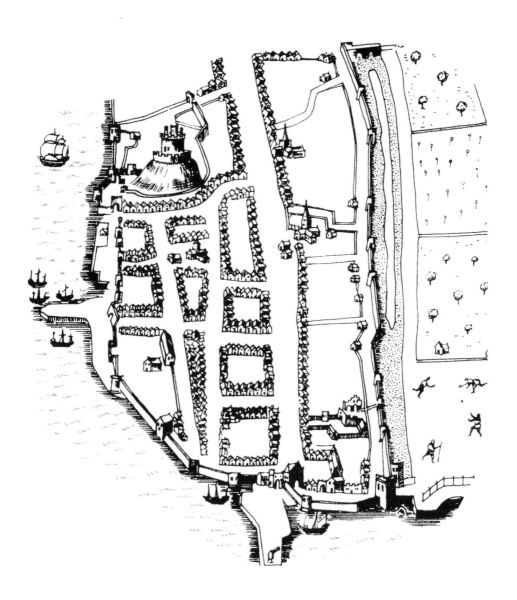

## PRE-DOCKS

That part of the coast where Southampton now lies has been used as a safe and sheltered haven since ancient times, while the rivers Itchen and Test have been used for communication between the coast, the hinterland and beyond.

Settlements are known to have been established in and around what is now Southampton from at least Roman times. These predecessors of the modern city changed their precise location over the centuries, depending perhaps on whether the inhabitants sought protection or communication, or the use of land on which to grow crops. The settlement of Hamwic was the main trading port for the City of Winchester, the main royal and ecclesiastical centre of the West Saxons which became the capital city of England before the Norman conquest of 1066.

The name 'Southampton' first appears before the Conquest. The Normans built their castle so that it overlooked the Saxon town of Hamtun and South Hampton was effectively a suburb to the south of this community. Both the castle and Castle Quay were constructed within a century of the beginning of Norman rule, although the first surviving record of the existence of the quay relates to its repair and dates from 1214. Some sources suggest that a harbour existed to the south-west of Chapel Tide Mill in the early thirteenth century and that when it silted up and became unsuitable for shipping it was modified as a pond to keep the mill operational.

West Quay appears to have been the next jetty to appear and was the centre of trade by the middle of the thirteenth century, followed by the construction of the Water Gate which is recorded as being new in 1411. This was obviously considered to be an important development in the capacity of the port as a trading centre as it was the location of the crane, a human-powered device using mechanical principles to move heavy goods. Ownership of a crane reflects the importance of Southampton as a trading port, as it was one of very few examples recorded outside London. The 'Accounts of Southampton Town' for 1449-50 first document details of its cost and upkeep. This crane, or its successor, had a chain substituted for a rope in 1816.

The loading and unloading of goods from ships and coastal craft was otherwise undertaken by licensed porters, who were formally organised as a distinct professional group in the late thirteenth century and who had agreed a set scale of charges for handling different cargoes at the port.

The Water Gate facility, sometimes referred to as South Quay, grew in stages. It was re-piled and paved in 1525, was lengthened in 1613 and then again in 1765. It was still known as Water Gate in 1821 when it received a gas light, supplied from the gasworks that had been established in Southampton the same year to produce the town's gas from coal. By the time the quay was extended again in 1853, it had become known by its modern name of Town Quay. It was widened in 1864 and extended several times during the next thirty years, although damage during the Second World War meant that the seaward end had to be rebuilt.

Continuing round the ancient shoreline in an easterly direction is God's House, a religious establishment based around the Hospital of St Julian, endowed in the late twelfth century as a refuge for the aged and infirm. Outside God's House was the Platform, built at the end of the thirteenth century and enlarged in the fifteenth century. This was later used to support a cannon as part of the town's defences, but its effectiveness diminished over time and the guns were replaced by a saluting battery in 1769.

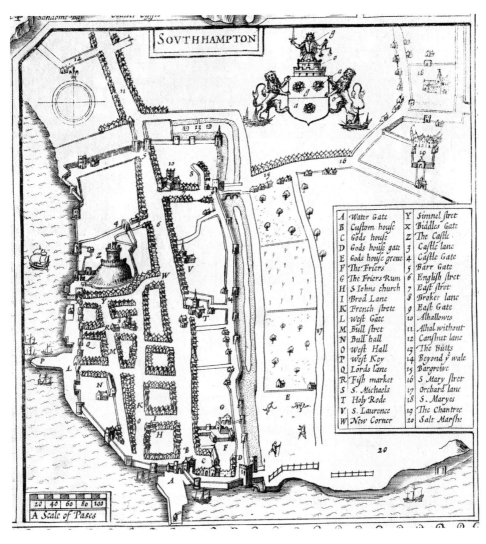

SOVTHHAMPTON

| | | | |
|---|---|---|---|
| A | Water Gate | Y | Simnel ſtret |
| B | Cuſtom houſe | X | Biddles Gate |
| C | Gods houſe | Z | The Caſtle |
| D | Gods houſe gate | 3 | Caſtle lane |
| E | Gods houſe grene | 4 | Caſtle Gate |
| F | The Friers | 5 | Barr Gate |
| G | The Friers Rum | 6 | Engliſh ſtret |
| H | S Iohns church | 7 | Eaſt ſtret |
| I | Brod Lane | 8 | Broker lane |
| K | French ſtrete | 9 | Eaſt Gate |
| L | Weſt Gate | 10 | Alhallowes |
| M | Bull ſtret | 11 | Alhal without |
| N | Bull hall | 12 | Carſhut lane |
| O | Weſt Hall | 13 | The Butts |
| P | Weſt Key | 14 | Beyond y wale |
| Q | Lords lane | 15 | Bargreive |
| R | Fiſh market | 16 | S Mary ſtret |
| S | S. Michaels | 17 | Orchard lane |
| T | Holy Rode | 18 | S. Maryes |
| V | S. Laurence | 19 | The Chantree |
| W | New Corner | 20 | Salt Marſhe |

20

20 40 60 80 100
A Scale of Paſes

*Above:* John Speed's map of 1611 showing the water's edge as it appeared at that time and the jetties at the Water Gate and West Quay. (Private collection)

*Left:* The Water Gate at the foot of High Street as it appeared in 1772. As it restricted access to what was later known as Town Quay, it was purchased by the Harbour Commissioners in 1803 and demolished a year later. (Private collection)

This print of 1773 shows the South Gate and Tower, better known today as God's House Tower. It has served both as the town gaol and as warehouse 'G' of the Harbour Board. It is now the Archaeology Museum. (Private collection)

So what was it that was coming and going from Southampton? After the Norman Conquest there was enhanced cross-Channel traffic, which by 1200 made Southampton the third largest port in the country. In the twelfth century the trade routes extended round the coast of mainland Europe, principally from Flanders (covering parts of the present day Netherlands, Belgium and north-eastern France) to Brittany, with lesser trade routes extending from Bordeaux in the south to the Baltic in the north.

The twelfth century also saw the beginnings of passenger traffic through the port, although not in the form we know today. In 1174 King Henry II had travelled from Normandy and landed in Southampton en route, via Winchester, to do penance at the tomb of Thomas à Becket in Canterbury. Other pilgrims from Spain and western France followed, and it is known that devout travellers to Europe and even the Holy Land travelled through Southampton.

Wool was an important element of the English economy at this time and was exported to Europe in exchange for luxury goods. Wool was sent out to Normandy, from where wine and stone were imported, and trade with the Channel Islands and Brittany involved the exchange of wool and provisions for stone. A less extensive trade dealt with the export of wool and supplies to Anjou, Poitou and Aquitaine on the western side of France, with wine as the return cargo. Timber was imported from northern Europe. By the middle of the thirteenth century these trade routes had extended to the Mediterranean, including links to Spain and Portugal.

Southampton is extremely fortunate in having buildings that still survive from this period which are able to convey something of the atmosphere of the time. Castle Vault is a good example of the storage facilities used to hold goods in transit through the port, while 'Canute's Palace', a house in Porters Lane, is indicative of the wealth of local merchants who grew rich on the proceeds of trade.

In the early part of the fourteenth century the principal commodities traded were English wool, which was exported, and wine, which was imported mainly from Gascony in south-western France. In fact, the medieval wine trade reached its peak during the early part of the fourteenth century with Bristol, London and Hull being the other principal ports involved. Tin and lead were coming into Southampton from Cornwall; cloth from Ireland; coal from the north of England; and wax, hides and flax from Spain.

A major development in the status of the port was the arrival of Venetian merchants who traded in high-value luxury goods, which they transported in oared galleys. The Venetians had a local monopoly in goods such as spices, silks, dyes and precious stones from the Levant or Eastern Mediterranean and, as a result, Southampton became a focus for the importation of such luxuries.

The French raid of 1338 had an immediate and lasting effect on local trade and prosperity. The town of Southampton was undefended along the southern shoreline as the local people preferred easy access to the port rather than the building of defences on the seaward side. Shortly after the start of the Hundred Years War with France, on the morning of Sunday 4 October 1338, a fleet of fifty galleys carried French soldiers and Genoese mercenaries up the Solent to land on the south shore of West Quay. The town was unprepared and unprotected and most of the townsfolk were in church. Even those citizens not at prayer and who fled to the churches for sanctuary were cut down. The invaders burned many houses, looted the town and stole the goods stored in the vaults, which included the king's own wine supply at the castle.

In the aftermath of the invasion King Edward III himself visited Southampton in 1339 to review the situation and ordered that walls be built to 'close the town'. Despite the losses sustained in the raid and the continuing war with France, there was a good deal of resistance to this plan on the part of the local merchant community. Apart from the cost of building and maintaining a wall between the town and the quayside, the wealthiest traders and ship owners had their houses fronting the port and were reluctant to lose their convenient and lucrative access to vessels coming in to the quays. As a consequence it took some forty years for the southern side of the town's defences to be completed when a wall was built in front of the existing houses, enabling the local traders to retain their properties on the waterfront while permitting defences to be manned on the upper level.

Trading activity was not entirely lost following the French raid. There was some revival in the hands of foreign merchants and the Genoese started bringing bulk cargoes such as alum (used as a mordant in the dyeing of cloth) to Southampton in large sailing carracks when previously they had used galleys to transport luxury goods. The Florentines also returned as traders to the port, but the wine trade declined until it reached its lowest point during the Great Plague of 1348-49.

The Tudor Merchant's House in French Street after restoration by English Heritage. (Bitterne Local History Society)

During the fifteenth century international trade continued, but mainly in the hands of foreigners. Galleys and carracks continued to come and, in fact, were sometimes laid up in Southampton for the winter. Wool continued to be exported to Venice with silk, spices, glass and other luxury goods returning. Wool also went to Genoa, Pisa and Florence, with sweet wine as a return cargo. This trade route also brought wine, wax, figs and currants from round the coast of Spain.

A shorter trade route brought wine and woad (used as a dye for cloth) from Bordeaux, salt from Nantes and iron, oil, leather and wax from Bilbao, with cloth and pewter flowing in the opposite direction. There was tin from Cornwall and canvas from St Malo; there were hides from Ireland and coal from the north of England, with fish also coming from the North Sea. Wool continued to go to Ghent and Antwerp; and the timber trade with the Baltic continued with furs following the return route from as far afield as Russia. There was also a flow of goods around the coast to London. A staple, or formally established centre for trade, for metals was established in Southampton in 1492. The vault at 94 High Street and the Wool House of 1417 are surviving examples of the buildings used for trade during the fifteenth century. These buildings, stone built and substantial, give some indication of the value of the commodities stored there and of the profits that were being made and ploughed back into the infrastructure of the port.

Even so, Southampton's great but declining international trade was almost extinguished during the sixteenth century. There was a prohibition on the Venetians exporting wool from the port in 1542. In 1551 there was an attempt to revive the free market in cloth and tin, but this failed, and while Southampton had a monopoly over the importation of sweet wine, which at the time came principally from Spain, this trade was never significant and had petered out by the 1590s. The maritime activity that remained consisted mainly of coastal traffic and trade with the Channel Islands and France.

The sixteenth and seventeenth centuries were periods of great religious upheaval throughout Europe. A group of people fleeing from religious persecution had sought refuge in Holland, but decided to seek the freedom to pursue their beliefs in the New World. The sea routes across the Atlantic were being opened up as explorers from Europe made their first forays into the New World and laid the foundations for transatlantic trade, beginning with such commodities as fur and fish from Newfoundland.

A postcard of the ancient Wool House at the corner of Bugle Street and Town Quay, with the Royal Pier Hotel next door. The hotel building was lost in the Blitz during the Second World War. (Bitterne Local History Society)

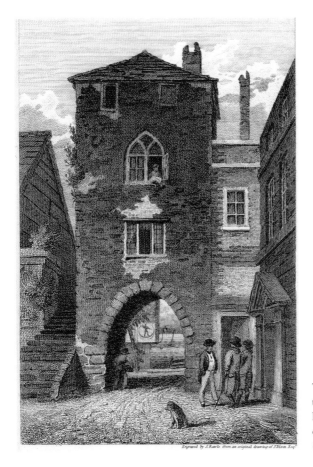

The West Gate in 1807, looking out
towards West Quay. The building
has lost its defensive role and been
converted into a dwelling house.
(Private collection)

The desire to colonise this rich and newly discovered continent was not new. Sir Walter
Raleigh had made an early, abortive, attempt to establish a settlement on the coast of
Carolina in the 1580s, which was followed in the early seventeenth century by the establishment of a colony in Virginia. This settlement was managed by Captain John Smith, on
behalf of the Virginia Co., and was ultimately successful. Smith's famous map of Virginia
was published at Oxford in 1612 and, taken with the news of the published accounts of
the earlier expedition, must have suggested to the European refugees that the Americas
were ripe for exploration by people with the courage and initiative to break away from
the repression that many were experiencing in the Old World.

Two of these refugees were despatched from their place of refuge in Holland to England;
Robert Cushman to London to arrange for the preparation of the ship *Mayflower*, and
John Carver to Southampton to procure supplies for the voyage. The *Mayflower* was then
brought to Southampton and anchored off West Quay around 29 July 1620. She was joined
by the *Speedwell* bringing the remainder of the refugees on about 5 August, but the vessel
unfortunately required repairs and the party were unable to set sail from Southampton until
15 August. Further difficulties meant that the pilgrims had to put in first to Dartmouth and
then to Plymouth, where the *Speedwell* was finally abandoned, and the *Mayflower* finally set
sail on 6 September. Despite the perils of the crossing, the Pilgrim Fathers eventually reached
their destination in what is now Provincetown, Massachusetts, on 11 November 1620.

Control of all the gates and quays of the early port, or what survived of them, was vested in a body known as the Harbour Commissioners, created by Act of Parliament in 1803. Its objectives were to administer the affairs of the port and unify jurisdiction over Southampton Water and its surroundings. The Town Clerk and one Thomas Nichols were appointed joint clerks at its first meeting on 18 April 1803. No time was lost in pressing ahead with developments and the report of the consulting engineer John Rennie was adopted in July of that year. The report proposed the construction of new quay walls flanking the Water Gate and the extension of the Water Gate itself in an easterly direction. In 1810 the dilapidated West Quay, which had been rebuilt in 1525 but had declined very much since, was auctioned off, any useful vestige of Castle Quay having disappeared long before.

Proper navigational aids were also an early subject of attention by the Harbour Commissioners. Old buildings were demolished and warehouses constructed, although for all this apparent dynamism the Commissioners were slow to embrace real change. They did go so far as to ask the Corporation for first refusal to purchase the mud land to the east of the Platform, but no action was taken regarding the provision of modern docks although the body had the powers, if not necessarily the funding, to develop the port. Even the original Parliamentary Bill of 1834, for the construction of the London & Southampton Railway, was initially opposed by the Harbour Commissioners on the grounds that it terminated too far from Town Quay, on which their attention was focused at the time.

In 1829 the Harbour Commissioners had to be petitioned by the townspeople to provide a pier. An Act of Parliament was obtained and the Royal Pier, initially a wooden structure, was opened by Princess Victoria on 8 July 1833. The new pier was an enormous success and was used by ships bound for the Isle of Wight, Normandy and the Channel Islands since it was accessible at all states of the tide. It was also used for recreation, as a promenade along the seafront and the pier had become a fashionable leisure activity for the middle classes who were able to watch the bustle and activity of a port that was still close to the heart of the town.

In 1863 an Act of Parliament constituted the Southampton Harbour and Pier Board as the Port Authority to take over the duties of the Harbour Commissioners. This was a public trust operating under private Acts of Parliament and its membership was both appointed and elected, with elections being held every three years. The Harbour Board was also the local Lighthouse Authority and the local Sea Fisheries Committee. It took on the maintenance of its own buoys in 1878, but it gained the power to levy light dues by an Act of Parliament only in 1882 and soon afterwards placed its first lightship at Calshot Spit to replace the existing buoy. A second, the Itchen lightship, followed near the southern extremity of the Empress Dock but was not in use for long.

The jurisdiction of the Harbour Board covered the whole of Southampton Water up to the causeways at Redbridge and Eling on the Test, to Woodmill on the Itchen, and to Bursledon Bridge on the Hamble. Since 1887, the southern limit had followed an imaginary line from Stansore Point to Hillhead and this boundary was extended by the British Transport Docks Act of 1972 to abut the Dockyard at Portsmouth and at Cowes Harbour. The Rochdale Committee, which looked into the operation of dock facilities throughout the country, had recommended to the government the creation of a single organisation for the control of port operations where multiple ones existed as an aid to efficient operation. Therefore, on 1 August 1969, the duties, functions, property and staff of Southampton Harbour Board passed to the British Transport Docks Board, which became the sole estuarial authority for the port. The Southampton Local Board was formed and first met in the reception hall at 102 Berth on 15 October 1968 to guide the Docks Board in the execution of its new role and to ensure a smooth transfer of responsibilities. Since privatisation of the Docks, Associated British Ports (ABP) has maintained these statutory responsibilities.

During the seventeenth and eighteenth centuries Southampton declined as a port until it was little more than a local harbour relying chiefly on coastal trade and with a limited share of foreign commerce. The port would not recover its former pre-eminence until the coming of the steam age.

From about 1750 the fortunes of Southampton took a different turn and were partially revived by its discovery by the Prince of Wales and his brothers as a resort and spa. Many large houses were built on the outskirts of the town by better-off people who wanted a country seat in this newly fashionable location. Following the development of these new and affluent suburbs, skilled artisans and tradespeople were drawn in to cater for the needs of the wealthy elite.

*Above:* Eling Quay in the 1930s. The scene is more tranquil than today, but there is still a lot of industrial activity with barges laden with telegraph poles and cranes handling ballast. (Stan Roberts)

*Left:* The Harbour Board offices, the second on this site, depicted as they appeared when used by British Transport Docks Board in about 1970. (Author)

High Street Below Bar in about 1860, showing All Saints and St Lawrence's Churches, as well as the coaching inns, the Star and the Dolphin. (Private collection)

Several gunsmiths, such as North, moved into the town, as did carriage builders like Andrews. Public baths where one could pay to bathe and benefit from the health-giving properties of sea water were built near the shore. The Assembly Rooms and a playhouse were established and the first banks and newspapers appeared in the town. It was also at this time that gentlemen of leisure discovered an affinity with the sea which they could express through the ownership and sailing of yachts. Their needs were catered for locally by the construction, crewing and maintenance of these vessels which were often substantial craft of 200 tons Thames Measurement. These were, of course, sailing craft in the early days, although in the nineteenth century the development of the marine steam engine meant that the steam yacht, a sort of floating palace, could become the object of desire for the gentleman amateur sailor.

Some idea of the yachting scene can be gained from the *Yachting World* description of Southampton during the spring of 1894:

> The forest of masts one has been used to see in our yacht-building yards during the 'saison morte' is getting thinner and thinner as various yachts are leaving their winter berths, and many a handsome and trim-looking craft can be seen lying either off the Town Quay or the Royal Pier here awaiting sailing orders.

The main yacht builders at this time were: Day, Summers & Co.; Summers & Payne from 1845; J.G. Fay & Co.; Mordey, Carney & Co. Ltd; and for smaller craft, John Pickett & Sons; H.R. Stevens Ltd; and Field of Itchen Ferry.

Southampton's yachting fraternity formed itself into associations to hold social functions and competitive events, as this was part of the appeal of participation in the sport. The original Royal Southampton Yacht Club was formed in 1837. The name was changed to the Royal Southern Yacht Club in 1844 to reflect its broadening membership and in 1846 the club occupied the building opposite the entrance to the Royal Pier, which is still an imposing landmark today. In 1947, the decision was made to sell the Southampton headquarters and remove to Hamble. The reason for this move was succinctly identified by the club as 'The Development of the Port of Southampton which has destroyed it as a yachting centre'.

A second Southampton Yacht Club, meanwhile, received its Royal Charter in 1875, becoming the Royal Southampton Yacht Club. Its clubhouse has been sited in various locations in Southampton, but since 1988 has been located in the marina at Ocean Village.

The origins of the Southampton Sailing Club go back to 1910 when Freemantle Rowing Club was founded. The name was changed in 1918, presumably to reflect a change in the activities involved, to Millbrook Sailing Club, and then became Southampton Sailing Club in 1957. It has occupied the present clubhouse at Woolston since the early 1970s.

The Motor Yacht Club was founded in Southampton by members of the Royal Automobile Club in May 1905. The club, established to cater for a new class of sportsman, had the title 'Royal' conferred in 1910. Its clubhouse was originally the former paddle steamer *Enchantress*, which was moored off Netley, but after various moves the Royal Motor Yacht Club moved to Poole, where it has been based since 1936.

Each of these clubs and societies has its own calendar of events which over the years have had varying degrees of prominence. The men who rowed coal out to ships in the River Itchen founded a rowing club in 1875 and their descendents still hold the Southampton Coalporters' Regatta in May for those dedicated to the sport.

Other developments were, however, taking place outside the port that would have an impact on the local economy. The River Itchen, which had been navigable up as far as Winchester in the Middle Ages, was improved by various cuts in the reign of Charles II to form the Itchen Navigation. This continued in use until 1870 when the sea lock at Woodmill that gave access to the navigable river fell into disuse, by which time Southampton and Winchester had been connected by rail.

The Andover Canal running from Andover to Redbridge was sanctioned by Act of Parliament in 1789 and opened in 1794. It was from this never-very-prosperous undertaking that a branch and an extension were begun which formed what was called the Salisbury & Southampton Canal. The branch from Kimbridge, north of Romsey, extended through East and West Dean to Alderbury and opened in 1803, but the last stage to Salisbury was never completed. The Andover Canal carried coal from the coast to settlements inland, with agricultural produce travelling in the other direction. The extension to Southampton would have had similar use, but it does not seem to have attracted much custom, perhaps because goods were already being transported in seagoing vessels along the coast.

The Southampton section of the canal continued from the point at which the Andover Canal ended at Redbridge, through Millbrook to the west end of the cliff face, which was later penetrated by the railway line beyond what is now Central Station. This part opened in 1802. The 880yd (804.6m) tunnel is slightly lower than, and at an angle to, the present railway tunnel, although they do intersect. On the eastern side of the tunnel the canal forked, with one cut going to a river lock at Northam and the other turning down the Ditches to a sea lock at God's House. Although the tunnel was constructed, it is not known if it was ever used and the Southampton stretch of the canal was abandoned in 1806.

*Above left:* The 'New Yacht Club', the premises of the Royal Southampton Yacht Club in Above Bar from 1885 to 1957. The tower faces Manchester Street. (Bitterne Local History Society)

*Above right:* Southampton from Millbrook Shore in about 1860, showing the Southampton to Dorchester railway line with the tunnel in the centre of the picture. (Private collection)

The remains of the canal were acquired by the Southampton & Dorchester Railway in 1845 and filled in to be used as the trackbed for the railway line from Redbridge. Likewise, the Andover Canal was purchased by the Andover & Redbridge Railway in 1859 and adapted in part for use by the railway.

## CREATION OF THE MODERN DOCKS

Meanwhile, a group of business people from a wide area – Manchester, Liverpool, London, Southampton and the west of England – were meeting in London to discuss the creation of modern docks in Southampton. These men, all of whom had interests in shipping and trade, put their proposal for the development of the port to the Harbour Commissioners in 1834. The initial plan was rejected, and a further approach was made in the following year. This was also turned down, on the basis that the Commissioners preferred to wait for more mature plans to be developed. Nevertheless, the Southampton Dock Co. promoted its own Bill through Parliament and was incorporated in 1836.

The first general meeting of the Southampton Dock Co. was held on 18 August 1836 at the George & Vulture Tavern off Lombard Street in the City of London. This set the pattern for twice-yearly meetings in February and August, although only the first five were held in the pub before the company moved its sessions to its offices at 19 Bishopgate Street. Conveyance of the land was completed by Southampton Corporation on 12 January 1837 and the company immediately pressed ahead with its plan to build the first dock.

The consulting engineer for the new company, and the man who had prepared the earlier plans, was William Cubitt, but the company's own engineer was Francis Giles. He was the son of the first construction engineer to the London & Southampton Railway and it is very likely that he recognised the potential for developing the railway and the port so that the function of each would support the other. Robert Mudie, in the first volume of his work on Hampshire, shared that view. Writing of the dock proposal, he thought it was a brave venture, but needed the combination of railway and dock together, bringing goods to and from London – an untried concept 'likely to be much more expensive than the proprietors appreciated'. He also thought that there was ample space for wet docks at Northam and therefore that the railway could have stopped there to avoid the expense of pressing on to the Terminus.

Queen Victoria's father, the Duke of Kent and Strathearn, had established the fashion for public Masonic ceremonies. There had already been such an event in Southampton with the laying of the foundation stone of All Saints Church in 1792, although not by the duke.

The inauguration of the new Docks was another such Masonic event. On the day of the laying of the foundation stone, 12 October 1838, there was a service at All Saints Church conducted by the rector, Revd John Emilius Shadwell. At the service, the sermon was preached by Revd William H. Brookfield, Provincial Grand Chaplain. Afterwards, the Mayor, Joseph Lobb, together with the Corporation and the directors of the Southampton Dock Co., travelled in procession down the High Street to the site of the proposed docks where Admiral Sir Lucius Curtis, Bt., Deputy Provincial Grand Master, laid the first stone.

This foundation stone was in two parts; an upper stone which was the one laid by Sir Lucius Curtis, and a lower stone which had a cavity in its centre, closed by a marble slab. In the cavity under the slab was a glass bottle containing ten coins, and under the bottle was a brass plate inscribed with the names of the distinguished people present at the ceremony. The plate read: 'In commemoration of the construction of commercial docks at the Port of Southampton, this foundation stone was laid by Sir Lucius Curtis, Knight and Baronet, of Gatcombe House, in this County…' The coins were a gold sovereign (£1) of 1838; a half-sovereign (50p) of 1837; a silver crown (25p) of 1821; a half-crown (12½p) of 1836; a shilling (5p) of 1838, sixpence (2½p) of 1837; a groat (nearly 2p) of 1838; with copper currency of a penny (just less than ½p) of 1826; a halfpenny of 1826; and a farthing of 1837. The currency was therefore not entirely that of the new Queen Victoria, but spanned the reigns of George IV and William IV as well.

Northam Wharf photographed in the 1890s from Northam Bridge. Gough's ice factory is in the distance and a timber yard, which later belonged to Gabriel, Wade & English, is in the foreground. (Brain collection)

Sir William Tite's Dock, later Terminus Station, in 1841. This shows the Dock House in the former Gloucester Baths in the background. Later the lower sills of the windows on the top floor of the station were lowered to cut through the projecting course of stones and a clock was placed on the balcony. (Private collection)

The Court of Directors of the Southampton Dock Co. had taken up residence in Dock House, its new Southampton headquarters, which was actually the former Gloucester Baths converted to offices. At a meeting on the day following the laying of the foundation stone, they resolved to present to Sir Lucius Curtis an inscribed silver trowel 'for the Honour conferred on this Company and the distinction with which he marked this enterprise by laying the first stone'. Joseph Liggins, the first Chairman of the Southampton Dock Co., was himself presented with a companion trowel to mark the occasion.

People then forgot about the very existence of the foundation stone until it was unearthed by workmen in June 1900 in its position fairly low down in the boundary wall. The contents were retrieved from the waterlogged cavity and sent to the headquarters of the London & South Western Railway Co. at Waterloo Station. Here they were displayed in the Directors' Room until they were loaned to Southampton Corporation for exhibition in Tudor House Museum. Unfortunately all the objects were stolen from the museum on 4 February 1929, although two of the coins and the brass plate were afterwards recovered near Town Quay. Replacements for the missing coins were obtained and the whole ensemble, together with Sir Lucius Curtis' presentation trowel and gavel, which had been acquired by British Railways in 1949, were then housed in the Dock and Marine Manager's Office in Southampton.

The lower portion of the stone, with the cavity, was incorporated into the boundary wall at the back of the Dock Post Office (near the present Dock Gate 4) and after moving to a new location, was identified by a plaque which read that it '… was transferred in 1951 to a position at the Ocean Terminal where it serves as a memorial to the pioneers who by their faith in the future of Southampton as a port, laid the foundation on which their successors have built so worthily'.

It has since moved again and now resides on the east side of Central Road, inside the present Dock Gate 4.

It so happened that William Bramstone Beach MP, who was a director of the London & South Western Railway, resolved to mark the progress made by the port by laying a coping stone at the south-west corner of the New Quays, which were then nearing completion, on the sixtieth anniversary of the laying of the original stone. The ceremony took place on 12 October 1898. This stone was inscribed and was happily united for the first time with the foundation stone at an event to commemorate the 150th anniversary of the original event on 12 October 1988. On this occasion, the staff were presented with commemorative nickel silver medallions.

Despite the ceremony associated with the commencement of the works, no great fuss was made about the actual opening of the dock facilities. The building site was visited by a deputation from the Peninsular & Oriental Steam Navigation Co. (P&O) in June 1840 to see if the planned facilities would meet their requirements. Further interest shown by the Royal Mail Steam Packet Co. (RMSP) actually changed the plans for construction and opening of the first element, the Tidal or Outer Dock. The original scheme, to open to shipping with the southern and south-east sides consisting only of sloping earth embankments, would have provided insufficient space for the new generation of steamship, and it was agreed that the whole of the dock wall would be completed before the dock became operational.

This change in plan extended the building period and delayed the point at which the Docks could open for business. Further difficulties were encountered in the construction work, as piling of the side walls proved ineffective and the whole had to be excavated and proper foundations inserted. The work was further delayed by exceptionally bad weather and by the discovery of fresh water springs that, together with the heavy rain, caused landslips. Francis Giles, engineer to the project, had predicted that the construction would be finished by 1 December 1841, but in fact the work took another six months to complete.

In the meantime, P&O inaugurated its mail service to Alexandria in June 1840 from the Royal Pier as the Open Dock was not yet ready. In August 1840 it was reported that the *Oriental* had run aground in the Solent. If true, it would have dealt a serious blow to the reputation of the Docks in Southampton, for it would have indicated that there might at times be insufficient water to support the claim that Southampton could be approached at any state of the tide. As it turned out, the *Oriental* had inadvertently dropped an anchor due to a cat-fall giving way, and this had been the cause of her coming to a halt. Her commander, John Soy, also commented favourably: 'It is my candid opinion,' he said 'that the Port of Southampton offers every advantage for steam navigation that can be desired for Steamers of the first class'.

The end of 36 Berth in 1898 showing part of the procession to the laying of the stone to commemorate the sixtieth anniversary of the founding of the Docks. The banner being carried by the dock workers is the one unfurled when Queen Victoria declared the Empress Dock open. Note that it says 'Southampton Docks L. & S.W.R.' around the coat of arms, although the Docks did not belong to the railway at that time. (Brain collection)

There were 600 men employed in dock construction during the winter of 1841, which increased to nearly 1,900 as the year progressed. Six steam engines and 150 horses were in use, as well as 500 tons of iron rails. Most of the work was in fact manual, as the steam engines seem to have been 'winding engines' that removed spoil delivered by the 'horse runs', while pumps removed the spring water. Despite all the setbacks, Giles' workmen were able to remove 19,000cu. m (25,000cu. yds) of material from the excavations each week.

Negotiations regarding the arrival of the Royal Mail Steam Packet Co. were also protracted. Parliament rejected the recommendation of the Admiralty that the West India Mail Packet Station should be moved from Falmouth to Dartmouth, and it continued at its original location until it could be transferred to Southampton.

Water was finally admitted to the unfinished dock on 18 May 1842 and the P&O ship *Liverpool*, with passengers and freight from Lisbon and Gibraltar, was the first to enter on 29 August. She was followed by another P&O ship, the *Tagus*, coming from London with the Southampton Dock Co. directors and directors from the London & South Western Railway, all of whom returned to London on an LSWR train.

The departure of the P&O *Hindostan* from the Docks on 24 September 1842 was an event of great celebration and attracted national attention, as she was the first P&O vessel to sail to India around the southern tip of Africa via the Cape. The ship then operated a regular service between Suez and Calcutta.

The new dock was finally opened to general trade on 1 July 1843 and once again a P&O ship, the *Pacha*, was the first to enter. One of the few other vessels to use the dock prior to its official opening was the sailing brig *Tartar* which arrived from London on 18 May 1843 to load, amongst other cargo, twenty brass cannon cast by the local cannon founder James Wolff for the Mexican government. According to *The Times*, she would have been the first ship to take merchandise from Southampton had the munitions that she was also carrying not exploded. The disaster occurred on the morning of Friday 2 June, setting the ship on fire and causing irreparable damage. The *Pacha*, which also discharged goods, therefore became the first ship to depart with cargo.

Giles had reported to the directors of the company that he intended to build the dock walls, which were of brick and concrete, up to the level of low water spring tides, and then he would let the water in and build them up to the full height in stone. This was partly to stabilise the structure, so that the water in the dock would help to support the walls, and also to make ready for the arrival of the Royal Mail Steam Packet Co. which had formed a favourable opinion of Southampton. John Smeaton had been co,mmissioned to advise the RMSP Co. and his report ended, 'Southampton as a Steam Boat Station is unrivalled in England'.

Francis Giles had already made the opening in the walls in readiness for the creation of the second, or Close Dock, which the Dock Co. was keen to progress as it was expected that this would 'yield the Proprietors the largest return'. There were minor setbacks; for example the dock gates floated off their pivots when the tide was admitted for the first time. However, this problem was overcome and there was a large crowd of spectators present on Saturday 6 December 1851 when the Close Dock opened. As with the Tidal Dock, there was no official opening ceremony, but the *Hampshire Independent* noted that 'Mr. Lamb's [the Chief Engineer of P&O] pretty little experimental steamer *Mary* led the way into the new basin at 11.00am followed by the Dock tug, having in tow the newly-launched ship *Hampshire*, and two colliers coming to discharge'.

Following similar thinking to that employed when the Outer or Open Dock was created, the Dock Co. had initially left the south and west sides of the Close Dock as gravel
slopes, but increasing trade caused the company to reconsider. Inner Dock, as it became,
was deepened by 4ft (1.2m), the entrance lock widened by 10ft (3m), and the previously
unmade quays finished in 1859. Following these improvements, the first ship to enter
was the P&O *Pera* on 20 May. She was greeted by the Mayor, who was accompanied by
members of the Dock Co. and representatives of the railway and shipping companies.

With the opening of the Great Exhibition on the horizon, the Mayor of Southampton
wrote to the President of the United States, inviting him to land his nation's contributions to the exhibition at Southampton. The Dock Co. was in full agreement and
offered a free berth as an inducement. The 2,000 ton sailing frigate *St Lawrence* therefore
anchored at Netley on 20 March 1851 to be met by the Dock Superintendent, Captain
Peacock, and entered the Docks to discharge her cargo the following day. Much was
made of the visit and even the *Illustrated London News*, which described the cargo, the
ship and her reception in two issues, spoke of her 'noble mission'.

The real benefit of the *St Lawrence's* arrival was in showing the international mercantile
community that Southampton had no trouble handling big ships. *St Lawrence* was not
the only craft to visit because of the Great Exhibition. The Turkish frigate *Feizi Baari*,
which also carried exhibits bound for the Crystal Palace, docked at Southampton and
was opened to the public on Sunday 27 April.

THE "ST. LAWRENCE" ENTERING SOUTHAMPTON DOCK.

The United States' contributions to the Crystal Palace Exhibition of 1851 arrive in Southampton
on board the USS *St Lawrence*. The items destined for the exhibition included examples of the latest
agricultural equipment, such as C.H. McCormick's reaping machine, which was thought by *The Times*
to be one of the most significant exhibits. (Private collection)

*Himalaya*, the largest ship in the world at the time, made her maiden voyage from Southampton on 20 January 1854. She too had previously been open to the public, an event which was widely reported in the press and helped to keep dock development in Southampton in the public eye.

Two factors are said to have influenced the consolidation of the growing trade of the Docks at this time. One was the award of a new government mail contract to the Royal Mail Steam Packet Co. to carry mail to Brazil and the River Plate in addition to its existing West Indies contract. The other was the creation in around 1847 of a large sugar refinery that was originally intended to supply the southern counties and some export markets with sugar refined from imported West Indian cane. The location of the business at Southampton must have appeared as a logical progression, for there had been a sugar 'house' in the town during the eighteenth century. In fact the refinery, built by Garton, Hill & Co., was used for the production of 'Sacharum', a patent inverted cane sugar used in the brewing industry. This was exported to Australia, New Zealand, South Africa and occasionally to India and the Continent. The manufacturers moved their business to Southampton Wharf, Battersea, in 1882 and ended the town's second link with the sugar cane industry.

All seemed set for the Dock Co. and the town to prosper, albeit in a fairly unremarkable way., and an extension to the dock was made. The size of ships continued to increase, but a large part of the company's land was undeveloped as they were unable to obtain capital for expansion. Conditions changed for the worse when P&O left in January 1882, and it was rumoured that the Union Steamship Co. was also considering leaving. Traffic was reduced further by the African wars in Zululand, the Transvaal and Egypt. The Dock Co., however, which for some time had contemplated the construction of another larger dock, was confident of an upturn in trade. The directors were minded to ask the Corporation if they could borrow the money with which to develop the dock, but there were dissenting voices in the town and they therefore entered into negotiations with the London & South Western Railway to subscribe a maximum of £250,000 towards the expansion project. A deal was struck and the contract for constructing this new deep-water dock was signed on 1 July 1886.

Independently, the Harbour Board commissioned a report into the development of the Docks and the engineer A.M. Rendel submitted his proposals in 1884. He had been asked to consider the need for and the method of development of deep-water berths, deep water in those times being 25ft (7.6m). Rendel appears to have been in no doubt that further extension was necessary. His preferred method of extension was to create solid quay walls forming a dock on the Itchen spit, which was already being partially developed at the time. These quays, he advised, could be either on the exterior of a solid promontory or on the interior faces of what would be an open dock. This idea was later carried into effect by the Dock Co. with the creation of Empress Dock in 1890, where eventually there were berths for ships on both the exterior and interior faces of the dock.

The Itchen Quays, which later became 30-33 Berths, had already been constructed between 1873 and 1876 on a spit of land that became part of the perimeter of the new dock. Although larger than its predecessors, work proceeded very quickly so that it was completed in only four years. Queen Victoria consented to open it, the first reigning British monarch ever to perform such a ceremony.

The Queen arrived from Cowes on Saturday 26 July 1890 on-board the Royal Yacht *Alberta,* which broke a ribbon across the entrance and then steamed round the dock to the West Quay, which is now 20-21 Berths. Here the Chairman and directors of the

Southampton Dock Co. boarded *Alberta* to be presented to the Queen and to deliver an address. After thanking them, the Queen responded that, 'It gives me great satisfaction to inaugurate this important addition to the enterprise of my kingdom. I trust that the Port of Southampton will feel the benefit of the great work you have completed and will exhibit in the future increasing developments of trade and prosperity'.

As soon as Her Majesty had expressed her pleasure that the dock should be named Empress Dock, a banner proclaiming the name was unfurled on the quayside to great applause amongst the 30,000 invited guests who had assembled in the sunshine.

Empress Dock made Southampton the only port in Britain where vessels of the deepest draught then afloat could enter and leave at any state of the tide. It was extensively used by ships of the Royal Mail Steam Packet Co., and the first ship to enter after *Alberta* was the RMSP's *Clyde*. She was followed by other famous steamers of the line such as *Don*, *Para* and *Nile*, which traded to the West Indies, and ships of the Union Steamship Co., such as *Gaul*, *Goth* and *Greek* with produce from Mauritius and Madagascar. The Union Line's steamer *Scot* made her maiden voyage from the Empress Dock in 1891.

Despite all these achievements, the Southampton Dock Co. was not doing well and was unable to repay the loan from the London & South Western Railway Co. to build the Empress Dock. The company was therefore taken over by the LSWR in 1892, an event which was curiously foretold by the mistake in the banner unfurled at the opening of Empress Dock and which proclaimed 'Southampton Docks, L. & S.W.R., Empress Dock'. Under railway ownership the development of the quays on the exterior of Empress Dock proceeded rapidly with the creation of the Extension or Prince of Wales Quay (34-36 Berths), followed by South Quay and the Test Quays.

## ALTERNATIVE SCHEMES

(Please refer to pp144-145 for the shape, size and location of these schemes, and their relationship to the Docks as actually built.)

It is useful to consider some of the alternative proposals for development of the Docks as they shed some light on the way the actual designs came into being. None of the following schemes were built as described, but were put forward as likely solutions to developing needs.

In 1724, Mr John Grove proposed an enlargement of the quays by the addition of two circular piers. He was encouraged by the Corporation, but the scheme fell through.

In a pamphlet entitled 'Commercial Docks on the South Coast of England', published in Southampton on 22 December 1835, a plan was put forward comprising four docks, of which the most westerly was to be unconnected to the other three. Mudie described this version of the plan in his work on Hampshire:

> It is proposed to form four docks, of about 14 acres (5.7 hectares) of surface each. Three of the docks are intended to open from the channel of the Itchen... And one dock is to enter from the channel of Southampton harbour... From a lock with double gates... But the three eastern ones are to consist of a receiving dock and two inner docks...

The authors of this scheme were: Captains Ward, Stephens and Forder; John Hunter, Lloyd's Agent and Surveyor; and the commanders of two ships, John Bazin of the *Ariadne* and James Goodridge of the *Lord Beresford*. They appear not to have been members of the Board of the nascent Southampton Dock Co., though Captain William Ward, RN, later became the Company Superintendent at Southampton. Nevertheless, it was said that their plan was 'being carried into immediate execution'. The accompanying text contains transcripts from the evidence given to the House of Commons in connection with the Railway Bill of 1834. Expert witnesses like Sir Thomas Hardy Bt thought Southampton better for mercantile purposes than Portsmouth.

The original plan for the Docks as advocated by Giles, the Dock Co. engineer, was to begin with a 'Western Dock' measuring 1,700ft by 500ft (518m by 152m, giving an area of 19.5 acres or 7.9 hectares), with its entrance from the River Test accessible through double lock gates, its long dimension being parallel to the landward part of Town Quay. In position, although not in form, this would have occupied the site of the later Ocean Dock. This plan was published in a pamphlet by E.L. Stephens, although it might be considered the 'official' version as it was endorsed by the Southampton Dock Office in London on 12 October 1838. It concluded that the railway system that existed or was in course of construction formed a spine down the whole country over which goods could be transmitted with ease to virtually all parts.

Finally, Messrs Cubitt and Mylne submitted a report to the Southampton Dock Co. at its offices on March 1839. This plan comprised four docks in a 'C' shape, all interconnected, as 'proposed by Mr Giles'. The third and fourth from the top were named 'Mr Giles's Western Dock' and 'Mr Giles's South-eastern tide dock' respectively. The compartments at the outer extremities of the 'C' were both to be tidal, with entrances accessible from the Itchen. The recommendation was that work should begin with the construction of what became the Outer Dock, and the report was approved at a Special General Meeting of the Proprietors of the Southampton Dock Co. at the George & Vulture on 18 April 1839.

In the end this scheme was not fully realised, owing in part to the financial circumstances of the company. Given Southampton's prolonged high tide, relatively modest tidal range and deep water to begin with, such features as the abundance of lock gates contained in the proposal were in any case unnecessary.

Subsequent to the opening of the Empress Dock, further developments were contemplated and the Transactions of the Institute of Naval Architects for 1895 show a plan put forward for the next phase. In the position of Ocean Dock and the Trafalgar Dry Dock, two smaller tidal docks lying on the same axes were proposed.

In fact, work started on the building on what was originally termed the 'New Dock' in 1906. It was generally known as the White Star Dock, as it was primarily to accommodate the White Star Co.'s largest vessels. Some of the material removed in its building went to reclaim the ground on which the Pirelli General cable factory was later erected. The contractors were Topham, Jones & Railton Ltd, the firm that subsequently went on to enlarge Trafalgar Dry Dock. This New Dock was officially opened, without much ceremony, by the sailing of the *Olympic* on her maiden voyage on 14 June 1911. The name of the dock was changed to Ocean Dock in 1922.

After the First World War, when the Old Docks had reached their fullest extent and further capacity for bigger ships was required, initial consideration was given by the London & South Western Railway to a scheme to construct new docks in Woolston. This was ultimately rejected as it was on the opposite side of the river to the existing docks and a suitable rail connection would have proved difficult. Subsequently, agreement was reached with Southampton Corporation and Southampton Harbour Board for a north-

*Above:* Two postcards combined to give a panoramic view looking inland and showing the construction of Ocean Dock in 1908. Trafalgar (No. 6) Dry Dock, completed in 1905, is in operation on the left and contains a White Star ship. (Author)

*Left:* West Bay taken from Forest View, showing the original quayside. The water's edge has now been pushed much further to the left and the land reclaimed. This became the site for Pirelli, and is now a vacant plot next to the West Quay shopping centre. (Brain collection)

westerly extension, incorporating the bay that had for so long been part of the landscape. In 1923 Parliamentary sanction was sought for this, the New Docks.

Even this new development was not without various changes from what is seen today as the final form. Two alternative methods of obtaining a longer quayside were contemplated. One appeared in the Southern Railway magazine *Over the Points* in March 1932, where the map showed a 'site for future jetty'. This was to be a structure parallel to the new quay wall and running for most of its length from 109 Berth to 102 Berth, connected to the land by a narrow continuation at forty-five degrees to the new quay, joining just to the east of King George V Dry Dock. An even earlier proposal contemporary with the approach to Parliament had been to construct a series of five jetties projecting into the Test from the present quay wall, also at forty-five degrees to it, running approximately north to south. The original approach to Parliament had been to construct a series of five jetties projecting into the Test from the position of the present quay wall. In this case, the two dry docks were transposed to the eastern end, next to the park. Both these plans for the Western Docks would have maximised the length of quays that could have been provided for shipping in the given area. In the last mentioned case, Southampton would have begun to look more like the waterfront at New York. However, even disregarding the cost of these schemes, there would have been difficulties involved in the day-to-day operation of the port.

The map referred to in *Over the Points* also showed the presence of a feature discussed in the original concept, the construction of a second dry dock of identical proportions to the King George V, parallel to it and a short distance to the west. This, of course, never came to fruition although an eighth dry dock for Southampton had been proposed after the Second World War. Trial borings in the mud of the River Test were made for this purpose in early 1958 between the westerly edge of the top swinging ground and Millbrook Point, but nothing ever came of the scheme.

When the British Transport Docks Board announced its proposal for a 'Westward extension project' for Southampton Docks in 1965, a plan was published which showed the fully developed area. There was a quay wall at right angles to the wall of the Western Docks, from the corner where King George V Dry Dock lies, and it was much as is seen today, but beyond that two indentations were proposed in what is presently the Container Port. One cut, a dock really, was to run parallel to the Western Docks between what are now 201 and 202 Berths, and another at forty-five degrees to the present quay wall, approximately between 206 and 207 Berths. This was proposed to give an extended surface comprising twenty-eight berths of 650ft (198m) and two of 800ft (244m). The emphasis was on cargo handling in line with the recommendations of the Rochdale Committee, which had foreseen Southampton developing as one of the country's principal cargo ports.

There were to be roll-on roll-off facilities at these new berths and 'there will also be an opportunity for experimenting with other new methods of operation as these develop over the next few years'. There would be transit sheds on the quays providing nearly 750,000sq. ft (69,750sq. m) for import and export traffic. In the March/April 1967 issue, *Docks* magazine reported on the announcement by Barbara Castle, the Minister of Transport, that the first phase of the Western Docks Extension Scheme was to go ahead immediately and published a revised plan for the whole development. In this, the principal alteration was that the first inroad into the new dockland would be parallel to the planned cut mentioned above, at forty-five degrees to the present quay wall, approximately between 206 and 207 Berths. It would breach the present quayside at approximately 205 Berth.

This time the first berth was to be of 1,000ft (305m) and was to be for container ships, with a 20 acre (8 hectare) container marshalling area behind. As the whole scheme projected further into the Test than the present docks do now in the region of the Bury Swinging Ground, the room for turning big ships as they emerged from these recessed docks would perhaps have been limited. This may be the reason for their non-appearance.

Plans for the post-war reconstruction of the cargo sheds lost to enemy action were announced in the 1947 *Dock Handbook*. It was proposed to erect two massive warehouses for general cargo, of which the one to be erected towards the western end of the New Docks was described in some detail. It was to be made of reinforced concrete and brick construction, 400ft (122m) long and 100ft (30.5m) wide, with a vault and five floors above ground level. It was noted that:

> The new warehouses will be built in the most modern manner and equipped with electric lifts and other appliances for the rapid handling of merchandise. They will provide cool vault accommodation for wines, spirits and semi-perishable produce, whilst the upper floors will accommodate general merchandise, both free and bonded, grain, tobacco, etc... Adequate railway tracks along one side and a lorry loading platform along the other will be provided...

In 1969, the British Transport Docks Board was considering the development of roll-on roll-off ferry services from Southampton and sought Parliamentary approval to provide such a berth by reclaiming the old Coal Barge Dock, which was then being used for timber barges. This would have created a berth in the River Itchen facing the Vosper-Thornycroft shipyard, although modern vessels would have had difficulty reaching it. Ro-ro berths have, however, been created further downstream.

# 2

# INFRASTRUCTURE

## POWER SUPPLY

In the early 1820s Southampton became one of the first dozen or so towns in Britain to install the new and innovative form of street lighting using town gas. The fuel was supplied from the local gasworks and the system was so successful it was extended to the Docks quite early on.

Apart from the steam-powered 100-ton sheer legs of 1861 and a 5-ton steam crane which had been bought from the Great Exhibition of 1851, there was no power-assisted machinery available to lift and manage freight, although there were some small hand-operated cranes.

In 1856 Southampton became only the third dock after Goole and Hull to employ hydraulic power, although in the beginning it was used only to power the drawbridge at the entrance to the Inner Dock. Nearly all the plant to supply hydraulic power, which was later extended to work many of the cranes, was acquired from John Abbot & Co. of Gateshead. A pair of tandem compound condensing steam engines were provided by Abbot, which were capable of supplying 300 gallons (1,364 litres) of water per minute at a pressure of 750 lb/sq. ins (5,171kPa).

Tracks were laid alongside the new docks and shunting locomotives and three pairs of horses provided so that goods could be moved by rail. Fresh water was conveyed round the Docks by pipe so that a supply could be provided as necessary to ships moored alongside by means of flexible hoses. This supply came from an artesian well which was 220ft (6.7m) deep. It was also a useful facility to have available in the event of fire.

When the British Association visited the Docks in 1882 electric light was laid on for the event which was hailed as 'a wonderful achievement', but the installation was only temporary and the company reverted to the use of gas lamps. The Harbour Board was first to use electricity as a source of power for the cranes on Town Quay in 1893, which therefore became the first electric quayside cranes in the country. It was only after the railway had taken over the Docks that the first permanent electric lighting was introduced in 1898. A total of 400 lamps were installed in the sheds round Empress Dock, the extension and 'other parts'. Twenty-five arc lights of 3,000 candle power were used on the quays, of which two were placed on those used by ships from American Line.

The Dock Co. generated its own electricity, using steam to drive the generating machinery which was provided from the boiler of a shunting locomotive outside the engine shed. This arrangement was, however, soon replaced by specialist equipment supplied by Willans Crompton. At 75ihp (56kW) this was said to be 'the largest in town'. Later on a generating station was added to the engine house of Dry Dock No.3, but this too proved to be inadequate for the purpose. It was replaced by the generating station comprising six dynamo sets attached to Trafalgar Dry Dock, which began service in 1905. There were overhead gantry cranes in a few of the sheds in 1903, which were followed by the 50-ton machine erected at Trafalgar Dry Dock in 1904. The grain elevators at Inner Dock were also electrically powered so that by 1910 the annual usage of electricity in the Docks amounted to some 1.6 million units.

A further eight electric cranes were commissioned at Ocean Dock in 1911, establishing a relationship with Stothert & Pitt of Bath which continued until the creation of the container terminal. The majority of the cranes supplied by the firm were of the level luffing type, so that once raised to the desired position the load remained at a constant height no matter what the radius of the jib.

The hydraulic cranes were all installed in the days of the LSWR and ultimately there were twenty in Outer Dock, fourteen in Inner Dock, eighteen in Empress Dock and four on Itchen Quays. Hydraulic power was extended to some dry dock gates and capstans, but in 1922 it was decided to replace steam and hydraulic machinery in the Docks with electrically powered equipment. Completion of the task was delayed by the Second World War and the last hydraulic crane, which was at 2 Berth in Outer Dock, was not dismantled until 1954. The drawbridge of Summers & Day at the entrance to Inner Dock had been converted to electrical operation at the end of 1953. The hydraulic mains were abandoned after the electrification of the caisson haulage machinery at Trafalgar Dry Dock in the summer of 1956.

The first heavy lift vessel employed in the port was the 150-ton *S.R. Floating Crane No.1*, built by Cowan, Sheldon & Co. of Carlisle in 1924. When not in use it was based at 48 Berth. It was originally steam powered, although it was never self propelled and had to be moved into position by tug. Like the tug tender *Calshot*, it went to work on the Clyde from 1941 to 1945 during the Second World War. On its return in 1946 it had a major overhaul and was converted to diesel-electric power in 1962, when the pontoon plating was repaired. Following further repairs in 1971 it was restored to its original capacity, having been restricted for a while in the load it was permitted to lift. *S.R. Floating Crane No.1* was in use for sixty-one years, but in April 1985 was replaced with a 200-ton heavy lift vessel bought from Wilton-Fijenoord BV. The replacement crane, which entered service in June 1985, was self propelled, although it often moves with a supporting tug. Its previous owners had named it *Mammoet*, but a competition among ABP staff resulted in it being renamed *Canute*. For a time in the late 1940s, British Railways also employed a 60-ton floating steam crane in the Docks.

In part, the decision to convert to electricity throughout the Docks was a consequence of the impending introduction of the Floating Dock, which required a 1,200kW power supply that was not then available. A bulk electricity supply at 6,600V alternating current (AC) was obtained from Southampton Corporation Electricity Department in 1924 and in-house generation of electricity at the Docks came to an end. The growth of the Docks saw a rise in the demand for electricity and both the storm water pumping station of 1932 and pump house of 1933 attached to King George V dry dock acted as sub-stations, taking their supply from the Corporation and supplying the Docks, which operated on direct current (DC), by means of rotary converters.

The management of the Southern Railway expected that industry would move south in the period following the Second World War, and particularly to Southampton. They had foreseen that the availability of electric power, which was cheap, clean and easy to supply wherever it was required, meant that major manufacturing industries were no longer reliant on the power of steam and so no longer had to be situated near a coalfield. Post-war reconstruction of the port allowed the power supply at Southampton to be converted to AC throughout the estate by 1958, with the exception of supplies to cranes and dry docks. In 1963-64 new electricity supplies delivered at 33,000V were provided to the Eastern and Western Docks and subsequently a third, similar supply was provided for the Container Port.

Nowadays there are standby generators in the Docks in order to maintain vital equipment such as radar and communications systems.

More efficient lighting was introduced in the Docks in 1961. First the lighting on roads was converted from tungsten to sodium in the Old Docks in January, followed by the New Docks later in the year. The new shed at 26-27 Berth became the first building anywhere in the Docks to be equipped with fluorescent lighting, also in 1961.

Electricity consumption at the Docks has continued to increase. In 1939 it was 13 million units per year and by 1973, in spite of the impact of the Emergency Power Regulations then in force, had reached 71.5 million units per year. In March 2009 the Docks announced a ten-year agreement with the Southampton Geothermal Heating Co.'s Combined Heat and Power Plant at Harbour Parade, near West Quay. This contract, to supply 55 per cent of the Dock's power needs, is the first such arrangement in the UK and means that more than half of the power supply can now be provided from a source that is both local and renewable. Southampton is on a relatively thin part of the earth's crust and the heat from the core of the planet can be transferred to water, which in turn is available to meet energy needs, including the generation of electricity.

## DRY DOCKS

The original builders of the Docks and the subsequent railway owners believed that they should offer ship repair facilities for the benefit of vessels using the port, particularly as there was sufficient locally based shipping to support it. No. 1 Dry Dock was opened on 11 July 1846 when the Dock Co. gave a 'substantial supper' to the foremen and workers who had constructed it. The P&O *Achilles* was the first ship to be accommodated. No. 2 Dry Dock adjacent to it was completed the following year. Southampton Dock Co. was well aware of the size of vessels attracted to the port and declared No. 3 Dry Dock, which was built by George Baker & Sons and opened on 18 December 1854, to be 'the largest for mercantile purposes in the world'. The company had been thinking of the need to accommodate the then enormous P&O *Himalaya* of 3,500 tons. In fact, the first ship to use the new dry dock was the General Screw Steamship Co.'s *Crocus*. Even so, Dry Dock No. 3 had to be enlarged less than thirty years later and was first used by the *Werra* on 31 December 1883, although reconstruction work had been completed some two months earlier. By this time, No. 4 Dry Dock of 1879 was already in operation and, because of its principal user, was informally known as the Union Steamship Co.'s Graving Dock. (The term 'Graving Dock' derives from the cleaning of the bottoms of vessels and is an alternative name for a dry dock.) The fifth dry dock was opened by the Prince of Wales, later to be King Edward VII, on 3 August 1895. Given the name Prince of Wales Dry Dock, it was the largest in the world at the time and the only dock in Southampton to be closed by means of a floating caisson as opposed to gates or sliding caissons. The caisson was manufactured by Rennie of London and could be sunk in the entrance of the dock to seal the opening when required.

The need for even larger facilities was foreseen by the London & South Western Railway Co. (LSWR), which wished to maintain its position in the forefront of dock design and development. In 1900 the company instructed its consulting engineer, Mr Galbraith, to design an even larger dry dock, construction of which was commenced by the contractors John Aird & Co. in 1901. Four years later, on Trafalgar Day (21 October) 1905, during the opening ceremony the Marquis of Winchester said, 'As His Majesty's Lieutenant for the County of Southampton, I declare this dock open and name it Trafalgar Dock'. The band struck up 'Rule Britannia', the Marquis was presented with the small gold padlock that he had unlocked symbolically to open the new dry dock and the Mayor of Southampton was presented with a facsimile. Less than ten years later, with the coming of the *Olympic*, even larger dry dock capacity was required, but as construction of a new dock would take too long, the enlarging of Trafalgar Dry Dock was authorised. Messrs Topham, Jones & Railton

completed this task in two years and it reopened on 4 April 1913 with the dry docking of
*St Louis*. A further modification, the addition of a lengthening notch at the closed end, was
undertaken in 1922 in order to accommodate the *Berengaria*.

After the First World War, the *Bismarck* was awarded to White Star under the reparations
scheme. It soon became evident that the ship, now renamed the *Majestic*, would require
an even larger dry dock. The solution adopted by the London & South Western Railway
was to commission an enormous floating dock, designed by Clark & Standfield and built
by Armstrong Whitworth & Co. Ltd Delivery of this 60,000-ton structure was delayed by
a boilermakers' dispute and it could not be delivered until May 1924. It was opened by
the Prince of Wales (later Edward VIII) sailing into the submerged floating dock on the
bridge of the paddle steamer *Duchess Of Fife* and breaking a ribbon. Afterwards *Arundel
Castle* became the first ship to be dry docked. During this period the railway companies
were reorganised and, in 1923, the LSWR was amalgamated with several smaller railways
to became part of the Southern Railway.

*Briton* of Union Line in No.3 Dry Dock about the time of the Boer War. (Brain collection)

Ocean Dock with Trafalgar Dry Dock in the distance. The nearest ship is the White Star *Homeric*, which came to Southampton in 1922, and there is no evidence of the Floating Dry Dock of 1924, suggesting that the picture was taken before that date. (Stan Roberts)

*Mauretania* in the Floating Dry Dock. (Stan Roberts)

Aerial view of the construction of King George V Graving Dock, between the parallel walls running diagonally across the photograph. The concrete monoliths forming the quay wall of the Western Docks can be seen in the top centre, with a dredger contributing towards reclamation of the area on the top left-hand side of the picture by pumping in dredged material. The entrance to the new dry dock is on the top right, between the dredger and the camera. (Bitterne Local History Society)

Although Cunard announced at the end of 1931 that construction of its then unnamed super liner was going to be suspended, work went ahead on a new dry dock so that it could be accommodated in Southampton. The site was dredged and piled and the construction work carried out by John Mowlem & Co. Ltd, assisted by Edmund Nuttall & Co. Ltd The new dock was opened by the King on 26 July 1933 and was at the time the largest in the world. *Majestic*, the vessel that had prompted the construction of the floating dock and was still the largest ship in the world, was the first to be dry docked in King George V Graving Dock on 19 January 1934. Later there was a commemorative stone placed on the spot where the King and Queen had performed the opening ceremony.

This most recent dry dock made the floating dock unnecessary and it was sold to the Admiralty at the outbreak of the Second World War and removed to Portsmouth on 24 February 1940. It remained there for nearly twenty years until it was sold to a Rotterdam firm, Rotterdamsche Droogdok Maatschappij.

Perhaps the last occasion on which all the seven land-based dry docks were in operation simultaneously was on 10 December 1949, when *Sind* of the Royal Pakistan Navy was in No.1, HMS *Orwell* in No.2, railway steamer *St Julien* in No.3, *Maidstone* in No.4, *Warwick Castle* in No.5, *Alcantara* in No.6 and *Mauretania* in No.7.

Within ten years the glory days of Southampton's dry docks had come to an end. No.1, left idle in the late 1950s, became a haven for swans. In December 1961 work began on the process of filling it in. No.2 was filled in during February 1966, while No.3 closed in 1971 and filling in began in September of that year, by which time Dry Dock No.4 had already ceased operations.

The use of dry docks was seasonal and at peak times, during the winter months when crossings of the North Atlantic were in abeyance, as many as 6,000 men could be employed on overhaul work. A concrete apron was applied to the eastern side of King George V Graving Dock in early 1962 so that it could be used more effectively as a wet dock in the summer. The 50-ton crane was useful for loading heavy items of cargo. For a time in the early 1980s the last and largest two dry docks were leased to British Shipbuilders. Most recently, the last dry dock to close was King George V Graving Dock when the caisson that had been built by the Furness Shipbuilding Co. Ltd of Haverton-on-Tees was found to have become unsound. There are now no dry docks in Southampton.

## DREDGING

The first use locally of a 'steam engine dredge boat' was in 1832, but the depth of water remained more or less as provided by nature until 1882, when the Harbour Board obtained an Act of Parliament to deepen the approach channels to Southampton. The work was completed in 1889 when Netley Shoal and Test Bar had been dredged to a depth of 26ft (7.9m). In 1893, the Board increased the depth of the channel to 30ft (9.1m) and in 1907 dredged further, to 32ft (9.75m). In 1909 the route into port on the seaward side of Calshot was dredged for the first time. *Berengaria* had a depth of 39ft (11.9m), so between 1922, when James Dredging took on the contract, and 1927, there was continuous widening and deepening of the channel, which then reached 35ft (10.7m). In 1931, Southampton Harbour Board initiated its largest dredging contract to provide a channel 1,000ft (305m) wide where possible, 38ft (11.6m) deep below Calshot, and 35ft (10.7m) above. The Second World War shelved plans for further dredging, but in 1950 the Dredging & Construction Co. Ltd was engaged for the restoration and improvement of the main deep-water channel. The material cleared from the channel, which amounted to about 2 million cu. yds (1,529,000cu. m) of soil, sand and gravel, was dumped on marshland between Fawley and Calshot.

Two things should be explained here. The first is that the depths quoted are standardised on what is termed Mean Low Water Spring, so that at high tide there is another 10ft (3m) or more of water. The second is that when the dock owners and the Harbour Authority were separate entities, each had separate dredging responsibilities. The dock owner was responsible for the bed of the Docks themselves and the water around the quays to a distance of 600ft (183m) or more. Thus, while the Harbour Board was engaged with Esso in deepening the approaches to Fawley in 1957, 1961 and 1963, it was the dock owner that initiated schemes such as the New Docks Extension.

R.E.V. James' business came to Southampton during the First World War and become James Dredging, Towage & Transport Co. Ltd in 1918. This company won the LSWR dredging contract in 1922 and received a considerable boost when working on the New Docks Extension which began in September 1926. While this was the largest civil engineering project in the world at the time, it was later superseded by an even larger project when work on the Western Docks Extension commenced with the raising of the first bucket of spoil in February 1967.

Re-use of dredged material has always been desirable and the formation of the Western Docks (New Docks Extension) was an excellent example. The dredged material that was extracted during the formation of deeper berths at quays was pumped over the new quay wall to build up and consolidate the ground behind. In similar fashion, some material from the enlarged channel and swinging ground off Dock Head was used to fill Inner Dock in late 1965. Previously, in 1957, dredged material from the Docks was used to form an area of dry land on the tidal foreshore at Dibden Bay, where it was pumped ashore from dredgers by the pumping vessel *Carnroe*.

Dredging, one of the most expensive elements of dock maintenance, is a constant process, either in order to maintain the existing channels or to provide improved facilities. The main channels into the Port of Southampton are to be made both wider and deeper and 201 and 202 Berths are to be excavated to give a depth of 52ft (16m) from 2010, with the spoil being deposited at the Nab Disposal Ground off the Isle of Wight. Both these projects are under the control of Associated British Ports.

## RAILWAYS

Although originally a separate concern, the Docks were built to serve and be served by the railway. Passengers and goods were mostly conveyed by rail and virtually every quay had rail access. At its fullest extent, there were 78 miles (126km) of railway line in the Docks, including 26 miles (42km) in the Western Docks.

The first shunting engine used by the Southampton Dock Co. was a vertical-boilered machine acquired in 1865. This was followed by a well tank engine in 1866. Later six 0-4-0 tank engines were purchased in 1872. Three of these were sold in 1879, and a further five were added, the last two, *Clausentum* and *Ironside*, being acquired in 1890. On acquisition of the Docks by the LSWR in 1892, the new owners decided to introduce a recent design of their own, the 'B4' class of 0-4-0 tank engine designed by W. Adams. Fourteen of the twenty-five produced were allocated to the Docks, the last being supplied in 1908, but all of which remained in service until the New Docks were opened in 1932. These were: *Alderney, Brittany, Caen, Cherbourg, Dinan, Dinard, Granville, Guernsey, Havre, Honfleur, Jersey, Normandy, St Malo* and *Trouville*. From 1908 *Ironside* and *Clausentum* were no longer used as shunting engines but to operate passenger trains to and from the Royal Pier and Terminus Station.

In 1932 the Southern Railway, which by that time owned the Docks, introduced some 0-4-2 passenger tank engines and 0-6-0 'E1' class shunting locomotives. Both of these were products of an absorbed company, the London, Brighton & South Coast Railway, as the Southern Railway had no modern design for a powerful, short-wheelbase, shunting locomotive of its own. Fortunately, during the Second World War, the US Army Transportation Corps imported quantities of railway equipment via Southampton in support of American forces. Among the imports was an advanced design of 0-6-0 shunting locomotive built by Vulcan Iron Works in Pennsylvania. Fourteen of these were purchased by the Southern Railway for use in the Docks immediately after the war. Of the displaced 'B4' class, two were scrapped, some sold and the remainder redeployed in other parts of the railway system. While reporting on the 'USA' class, as it became known, dock literature of the time commented helpfully that it would make a 'homely impression for visitors from the US'. These engines were in turn replaced by diesel-electric shunting locomotives in 1962.

During the construction of the New Docks, the Dock Engineer's Department purchased an 0-4-0 saddle tank steam engine for its own use from Woolwich Arsenal. This was *The Master General* and it was itself replaced by an 0-4-0 Fowler diesel in 1946.

While there was extensive movement of goods on the internal railway lines, there were no fixed signals to control movements, except for the semaphore signals at Gate No.3 for joining or leaving the main line. These have since been replaced by colour light signals. A shunter was in charge of railway traffic and was responsible for setting points by hand and protecting pedestrians and vehicular traffic. In order to achieve better use of the locomotives, radio telephone equipment was installed in January 1956 for communication with Docks Traffic Control. The only visible difference was that aerials sprouted from the cabs of the engines, but the shunters continued to operate as before.

The Docks were also divided into 'yards' for the purpose of controlling movement. The New Docks were divided into East and West Yards and the Old Docks comprised Front Yard, Back Yard, Empress Yard, Ocean Quay Yard and Empress Dock Marshalling Yard.

It is said that during the First World War so many military trains were passing through Southampton that the level crossing gates were permanently closed against road traffic. An additional line was laid from what is now the Central Station, down Western Esplanade to a new military pier where rail traffic could be shunted directly onto ferries. This system remained in use for some time after the war for the return of equipment and the remnants of this pier were not finally lost until the beginning of the New Docks in the early 1930s.

West Station Southampton, now known as Central Station, seen from the south side and the down line in about 1900. (Bitterne Local History Society)

Special circumstances aside, it is difficult to determine what the general flow of traffic by rail was, as figures that are quoted for a special day, week or month are misleading. However, during 1962 there were 1,837 boat trains carrying 315,850 passengers into and out of the Docks, and also 5,282 freight trains. These figures had declined by 1968 to 847 boat trains conveying 196,743 passengers, and 3,737 freight trains. Possibly the greatest daily total in peacetime was achieved on 3 August 1951 when there were twenty boat trains to and from London and nineteen freight trains, with twenty-nine ships arriving or sailing.

Special rolling stock was constructed at Eastleigh for the magnificently appointed 'American Eagle' boat train which met passengers disembarking from the *New York*, the first American Line ship to dock in Southampton, on 4 March 1893. Boat trains were often named and new locomotive headboards were added proclaiming the 'South-American' for Royal Mail and the 'Holland-American' for Holland America Line in 1954, followed by the 'Springbok' for Union Castle ships in 1958. The carriages had roofboards with the name of the company and the words 'Ocean Liner Express'. All boat trains included Pullman stock for those wishing and able to pay for added comfort. The New Docks included a carriage cleaning and warming shed which opened in January 1936 and that could accommodate six complete boat trains. An unforeseen consequence of the changeover to diesel-electric shunting engines necessitated the introduction of special steam heating vans for the carriages.

The railway owners of the Docks were rather late in exploiting their unique position as both railway and dock owners, for the first rail excursion to see the world's largest ships took place only in 1927. Two years later there were forty of these specially arranged visits. They were revived after the Second World War and incorporated a two-hour cruise of the Docks operated in conjunction with the Southampton, Isle of Wight & South of England Royal Mail Steam Packet Co. Ltd (now Red Funnel). Educational rail excursions were added to the post-war repertoire with as many as 13,000 children being brought to the Docks in a year. These continued into the mid-1960s.

The first twenty of a new class of express passenger locomotives were delivered to the Southern Railway during the Second World War, beginning with the first arrival in February 1941. The company plan of naming these Merchant Navy Class locomotives after famous shipping companies was, according to the literature, 'a gesture of esteem to the officers and men of the Merchant Navy who preserved our vital lifelines during the war'. The later engines, delivered after railway nationalisation, had official naming ceremonies. Most of these were held in Southampton Docks in order to maximise the opportunities for publicity. The last to be named was *Ellerman Lines* on 1 March 1951. *Clan Line* and *Lamport and Holt Line* had already been named on 15 January the same year.

On the main line, diesel locomotives had been used for both passenger and goods trains since 1962 and electrification of the London-Bournemouth line was completed in July 1967. Many internal lines were now removed, the track from Terminus Station to Town Quay, laid by G.L. Emmett in 1847, was lifted in 1952 and the Terminus Station itself was closed to passenger traffic on 5 September 1966. However, Town Quay was still accessible from the Docks by rail until 1970 via a line that ran behind the Dock Post Office.

The ability of the railway to handle large quantities of goods was taken into account during the planning both of the Western Docks Extension and for the Dibden Bay development. By the late 1990s some twenty container trains per day were leaving the two Railfreight distribution terminals and this has increased to twenty-five, although the Millbrook Freightliner Terminal is currently out of use. In 2001 the Strategic Rail Authority announced its plan to invest in new capacity on the line from Southampton to

the West Midlands, enabling bridges and tunnels to be adapted to handle larger containers that could then be distributed from the port using the rail network. There are today
4.1 miles (6.6km) of railway lines in the Western Docks and 2.1 miles (3.4km) in the
Eastern Docks, with rail transport again growing in significance.

## ROADS

Roads were of much less importance than railways during the early years of the commercial docks and this continued to be so for some time. Roads were, of course, necessary
for day-to-day access and communication, although the length of the road system in the
Eastern and Western Docks amounted only to about 10 miles (16km) in 1950.

As with all elements of the estate of the Southampton Dock Co., identifying marks were
few and far between. The berths for ships had no numbers, neither did the accesses from
the town, and the roads had no names, or at least no official names. For convenience, unofficial names were soon adopted by those who worked in the Docks. Some of these names
were Ballast Road, Iron Fence Road and Gun Road. This state of affairs continued into the
ownership of the Southern Railway and it was only in January 1926 that the *Shipping Guide*
proclaimed that 'all thoroughfares in the docks have now been named'. This, of course,
referred only to the Old or Eastern Docks as none other existed at the time.

Until about 1990, if one imagined entering the Eastern Docks from the present Dock
Gate 4, one entered Central Road leading ahead and to the south. Very shortly one came
to a crossing – now a roundabout – with Boundary Road. When first named this encompassed the perimeter of the Docks, running east and west. The western arm on the right
was renamed West Road in the major renaming of September 1951. When created it had
been known unofficially as Gun Road, perhaps because of its proximity to the Platform.
Continuing along Central Road, Atlantic Road was on the right, running to the north-
west corner of Ocean Dock, with Trafalgar Road running down the east side of Trafalgar
Dry Dock, and further along Central Road, Brazil Road (Iron Fence Road) appeared on
the left. This ran along the back of the sheds on the north side of Empress Dock and at
the end joined at right angles with Java Road (Ballast Road), running along the back of
the sheds in the northern part of Itchen Quays.

A photograph taken after the
introduction of electric light in
1898 showing the unnumbered
road and rail access to the Docks
almost opposite the South Western
Hotel. The pillars to the left of the
picture, forming what was part of
the boundary between Inner Dock
and Canute Road, still exist. (Brain
collection)

Just beyond Brazil Road, going further into the Docks, was a fork. Diverging to the left was Empress Road passing to the west and south sides of Empress Dock, and to the right was Ocean Road running to the back of the buildings that flanked Ocean Dock. Prior to 1951 this was Cunard White Star Road and, before that, White Star Road. Ocean Road ran into Test Road along Test Quays and Empress Road linked with Itchen Road (Castle Road until 1951) following the west side of Prince of Wales Dry Dock before uniting with Test Road near the southern extremity of the Docks. If we returned again to the Boundary Road junction and turned east, Old Road on the right swept round the western and southern sides of Inner Dock and ended in another curve, Graving Road, running round the south and east sides of the first three dry docks. Inner Road ran along the north side of Inner Dock and became Channel Road, passing behind the sheds on the north of Outer Dock. Boundary Road continued east following the rear of the buildings fronting Canute Road, beyond Dock Gate 2. It became known as East Road from 1951.

From early 1967, also leading from Dock Gate 2, Melbury Road was constructed round three sides of the filled-in Inner Dock. Also from 1951, the Cunard Baggage Store was in Harcroft Road and the premises of Burnyeat, Dalziel & Nicholson were, appropriately for a ship's chandler, in Chandler Road. Central Road only became 'central' when the Eastern Docks reached their fullest extent. Otherwise the derivation of the names of roads is obvious. Most relate to nearby activities: Channel Road – ferries; Brazil Road – Royal Mail. Melbury Road takes its name from the headquarters of the British Transport Docks Board.

As presently constituted, Central Road remains the spine but there has been some realignment and renaming in the past decade. On entering Dock Gate 4, Maritime Way, formed from parts of Melbury Road and Boundary Road, now joins Central Road on the left, while slightly further on, Atlantic Way is encountered on the right-hand side slightly further along than the old Atlantic Road, and Atlantic Way runs into Cunard Road, formerly Trafalgar Road. Continuing along Central Road, what was formerly Old Road now intersects Central Road on the left and has been renamed European Way.

The plan of the Western Docks was much simpler and the main roads consisted of two running parallel to each other and to the quayside. Herbert Walker Avenue was the most southerly, behind the quayside buildings, and West Bay Road was further inland. These were joined by Solent Road at the eastern end. At the western end, running from Dock Gate 12 to the head of King George V Dry Dock, is Western Avenue, which was only named in 1958.

Test Road, when built, was one of the first concrete roads in the country. There were, however, few other innovations. Following a suggestion of the Divisional Police Superintendent, an experimental temporary roundabout was constructed at the junction just inside Dock Gate 10 in the summer of 1961. The experiment proved a success and Baillie & Edwards were awarded the contract to make this permanent in December 1964. Other roundabouts to control the flow of traffic followed in the Old Docks in the following year, with one just inside Dock Gate 4 (then known as Dock Gate 2) that has recently been reinstated. Another was built at the north end of Ocean Terminal at the junction formed by Empress Road, Ocean Road and Central Road with a link to Brazil Road, and yet a third followed at the junction of Old Road and Melbury Road in 1967. On 1 March 1957 the first speed limit, of 20mph, was introduced throughout the Docks, increased to 30mph in November 1965. A car park for 300 cars was created on the reclaimed land of Inner Dock at this time. The only other car park then available was for seventy-five vehicles on the south side of Boundary Road, opposite Maritime Chambers.

For a long time the Docks had little impact on the external road system. However, the Rochdale Report on the development of the country's ports had said in 1964 that expansion in Southampton must go hand in hand with improved communications with London, the Midlands and the West. This theme was reiterated by Sir John Fletcher-Cooke, MP for Southampton, speaking in the House of Commons in 1965: 'If money is to be spent on improving Southampton Docks, it must be accompanied by an appropriate expenditure on communication which brings cargoes to the docks for export'.

In late 1967 the Minister of Transport, the Rt Hon. Barbara Castle, announced that the government was making a bid to improve communications with the rest of the country by entering into a massive road building programme in Southampton and Hampshire. Work had already started on the Kingsworthy Link Road, a new bypass which was intended to eliminate the passage of heavy goods vehicles between Southampton Docks and the Midlands from the medieval streets of Winchester.

Following the creation of the first container berths, the British Transport Docks Board announced in late 1970 that it was going to construct a bridge carrying a two-lane dual carriageway across the main London to Bournemouth railway line to provide access for vehicles to the Docks. Southampton City Council likewise announced its intention to improve the road to the Millbrook roundabout to the same standard. A plan was now in hand to allow the growing road traffic to the Docks to link to the expanding trunk road system and bypass Southampton city centre. Weighbridges for the inspection of lorries and containers entering the Container Terminal were added at the same time and it was decided to designate the new Dock Gate as No. 20. A part-load transfer system was introduced to reduce congestion caused by heavy goods vehicles. The Nursling Link Road (M271) was under construction when the bridge opened in 1972 and this last piece of the jigsaw allowed road traffic easy access to both the M27 and M3.

Changes to the status of the various gates are best understood by referring to the following tables:

Changes to road access to Docks, May 1967
(with introduction of Swedish Lloyd's car ferry service)

Gate No.2 and Channel ferry gate remain TWO-WAY,
Gate No.5 is OUT instead of IN and
Gate No.7 is IN instead of OUT.

Renumbering of Dock Gates relating to road traffic: 20 April 1968

| | |
|---|---|
| Channel Ferry Gate | became No.1 |
| No.7 | became No.2 |
| No.5 | became No.3 |
| No.2 | became No.4 |
| No.1 | became No.5 |

Western Docks Gates 8, 10 and 12 remained unaltered.
With co-operation of Harbour Board,

| | |
|---|---|
| Town Quay | became No.6 |
| Entrance to Royal Pier | became No.7. |

As the rail crossing into the Docks in Canute Road was and is termed No.3 gate in railway literature, there was a time when there were two No.3 gates.

## BUILDINGS

The construction of buildings such as passenger terminals, dry docks and the quayside berths have been covered elsewhere. Other buildings that form or have formed a significant part of the built environment, and would otherwise slip through the net, are covered here.

The most important are the administrative headquarters. The first local building used by the Southampton Dock Co. was the converted Gloucester Baths, although the site was later taken over in 1847 for use as the Custom House.

The new company headquarters, Dock House in Canute Road, was completed in 1872. This building still exists, although it has been divided to form a branch of the National Westminster Bank at the east end and a pub, the Admiral Sir Lucius Curtis, at the west. The wall carries the railway company war memorials to local staff killed in both World Wars.

In December 1962 a new Dock House was completed for the British Transport Docks Board, bringing all the administrative staff under one roof for the first time. The initiative lasted only a few years before the accounts department moved out in 1968. The building was a flat-roofed reinforced concrete structure of five floors facing Canute Road, with a basement plant room and storage area. The main elevations consisted of double-glazed anodised aluminium panels and the ends were of reconstituted Portland

The Dock Co. offices of 1872 in Canute Road. It is now part bank and part public house – the Admiral Sir Lucius Curtis – and carries the memorials to staff lost in both world wars on the wall on the left, just out of view. It continued as the main dock offices until the building of the five-storey replacement opened in December 1962, which was further down Canute Road to the west. (Author)

stone slabs, with the area of the front door being surrounded by black marble. The architect, C.B. Dromgoole, was also the designer of the Ocean Terminal which opened in 1950, and the builder was John Laing Construction Ltd It has been replaced by an apartment block.

The present port offices were relocated to be nearer the centre of port activity in the Ocean Gate building adjacent to Ocean Dock. This was opened in September 1991 by the Lord Lieutenant of Hampshire, Lt Col. Sir James Scott, Bt, at which he unveiled a sculpture by Jenny Martin in the main reception area. This complements the restored Southern Railway centenary globe which is located outside the building. The architect of the new offices was Trowbridge Steele, and the builders Brazier Design & Build.

The offices of Southampton Harbour Board that can be seen today were erected in 1925. They had been planned for construction at the beginning of the First World War but were delayed for ten years because of the conflict. The building replaced the former offices on the same site that had been there since 1886, and which had been constructed on land reclaimed in 1879. The design of the new building was that of the Board's Surveyor, Mr. E. Cooper-Poole, and the builders were H. Cawte of Southampton.

The new Harbour Board offices were opened by Admiral Earl Jellicoe on 8 September 1925. The punctual arrival of Jellicoe meant that the padlock he was intended to unlock to represent the symbolic opening of the building was not in place, but it was presented to him as a souvenir in any case. After the ceremony, the new offices were opened for the public to view. The *Southampton Times* extolled the building, particularly its sumptuous panelling which, in part, had a suitably nautical theme for it incorporated fourteen high-relief carved panels from the White Star liners *Teutonic* and *Majestic*. These had surrounded the domed glass lights in the saloons of the ships and were acquired from the auctioneer and antique dealer William Burrough-Hill. One was placed on the stairs, with four round the base of the dome and nine in the Board Room. The building was extended in 1957 and, following the fusion of the Harbour Board with British Transport Docks Board, it was modified to accommodate the accounts department which moved in during November 1968. The building is now Maxim's Casino.

In the early days of the Docks, P&O handled around half the imports and exports passing through the port. So close was the association of the company with the town that the P&O School was opened in Paget Street in 1862 for the children of P&O crew and land-based staff. This later became one of the Corporation's Eastern District schools and then part of the technical college. It has since been demolished.

P&O was also commemorated indirectly through Andrew Lamb, its Superintendent Engineer, who gave part of his Belle Vue estate for the building of St Andrew's United Reformed Church in Brunswick Place. This was opened in September 1853, with the Lamb Memorial Hall being added in 1884. The site has since been redeveloped.

In 2002 ABP created Redbridge Wharf Park from 4 acres (1.5 hectares) of redundant railway land at the western end of the Container Terminal and populated it with 9,000 trees and shrubs of species native to Britain. The exceptions were the row of North American conifers which were planted to symbolise the timber imported at the old wharf to produce railway sleepers. A preserved crane sits on the park's waterfront to complete the historical associations.

The Royal Pier was created by the Harbour Commissioners in response to public demand and was opened by Princess Victoria in 1833. Originally of wood and built by William Betts, it was not initially intended for pleasure but was to provide a deep-water berth for ships trading with the Channel Islands and France, and was the initial departure point for P&O steamers. In 1871, after this shipping activity had transferred to the Docks, it was widened and extended. Railway lines were laid and a small pier station provided on the eastern side to handle traffic for pleasure and excursion steamers.

The design of the Harbour Board's Surveyor, Cooper-Poole, was selected for a further redevelopment of the pier which was opened by the Duke of Connaught, a son of Queen Victoria, in 1891. The first pavilion for entertainment was added in 1894 and the pier remained a popular venue for many years. In the 1950s it was handling 600,000 boat passengers a year, while 400,000 promenaders used its other facilities. The original gatehouse was enlarged in 1888 and was replaced by the existing domed structure in 1928, by which time the railway lines on the pier had been removed. The lions round the parapet are, however, a remnant of the original building.

As well as catering for pleasure seekers, the pier continued to serve as a ferry terminal for local commuters and became the location for the first commercial hydrofoil operation in the country when Red Funnel introduced the *Shearwater* on 2 May 1969. This reduced the journey time to Cowes on the Isle of Wight from around an hour to twenty minutes. Among its attractions, the pier also had one of the few post boxes introduced during the brief reign of Edward VIII. Maintenance of the structure, as with all other piers, was considered a problem and the pier finally closed to the public on 31 December 1979. Sadly the main structure was damaged by fire in 1987 and 1992 and its future remains uncertain, although the gatehouse continues to function as a restaurant.

The original Royal Pier that had been opened by Princess Victoria, as it appeared in about 1835. This wooden structure was designed by Doswell and constructed by William Betts. (Private collection)

The Pavilion on the Royal Pier, constructed in 1894, and photographed from the West Landing Arm. (Bitterne Local History Society)

The Royal Pier as it is today. The 2009 Boat Show is in process of being assembled in the background and *Red Eagle*, a Red Funnel vehicle ferry to the Isle of Wight, is on the right. The rectangular building in the background is the Holiday Inn Hotel, which was originally the Skyways Hotel. (Author)

## COMMUNICATIONS

From early in the nineteenth century the Harbour Commissioners developed a system for marking the approach channel to the port with booms. These floating spars were difficult to see and were hardly an aid to navigational safety. The Harbour Commissioners were, however, far-sighted and located an experimental navigation buoy, designed by Captain George Peacock, at Calshot Spit in 1851.

By 1926, the approaches were said to be illuminated by numerous gas buoys to make them more effective at night or in inclement weather. A signal station was erected at Calshot in the late 1920s in order to give advance warning of shipping movements.

At the Dock Head Signal Station, located at the most prominent point of the Old Docks, the arrangements for controlling ship movements had been much the same for many years. Shipping movements in and out of the dock, as well as other information such as the weather, were recorded in a ledger. A signalman hoisted flags to give instructions to vessels and the berth that an incoming ship was to use was displayed in black numerals on a white board. There were other features of this signal station that are worth noting. There was a signal lamp and storm cones that could be hoisted to indicate impending bad weather, and a bell that revealed the position of the signal station in fog; this was replaced by a foghorn only in March 1949. Repeat signals to ships were also given at 4 Berth in Outer Dock, 24 Berth at Empress Dock, 47 Berth at Ocean Dock and at 101 Berth in the New Docks, so that a vessel was sure to be directed to the correct berth. All this was soon to change. The Harbour Board, ever receptive to new ideas, was interested in the prospect of using a shore-based radar scanner for the supervision of Southampton Harbour and was able to use the radar-equipped HMS *Starling* to assess the potential of such a system in November 1946. Earlier that year, the Board had also indicated in the press its intention to carry out tests in the use of radio telephony to assist port traffic control, which at that time also included the control of aircraft movements to and from the flying boat terminal. These proposed developments were very much needed, as the *Queen Elizabeth* had become stuck on the Brambles Bank in April 1947, while Commodore Henry Manning of the *America* had criticised this way into Britain as being 'primitive' during the same month.

Calshot Castle became the new Harbour Board control station for the establishment of radio telephone contact between important shore points and ships arriving or sailing. This round-the-clock facility was known as the Port Operation and Information Service and the VHF radio element became operational in 1953. The same visual signals to ships, relating to the berth they were to occupy and whether or not they could enter harbour, continued to be used here as at Dock Head, for this was the accepted way of communicating with ships entering port.

In order for there to be successful two-way radio communications of the sort envisaged by the Harbour Board, both parties need to have the same equipment. A contemporary advertisement of the International Marine Radio Co. Ltd states that 'the Cunard liners *Queen Elizabeth*, *Queen Mary* and *Caronia* were prepared for the inauguration of this service… [by International Marine Radio]'. The need for and advantages of VHF radio communications gradually spread. One obvious outcome of this is that the Docks have become quieter, for big ships and their escorting tugs no longer need to communicate with each other by means of hooter and siren. The Port Operation and Information Service took some time to become fully functional with its harbour surveillance radar, but when officially launched by Harold Wilson, the then Minister of Transport and Civil Aviation, on 17 January 1958, it was the first such comprehensive service in the world. As part of the system, a new patrol launch, *Triton*, was brought into service to replace *Patrol 1*. It was equipped with radar, echo-sounder and radio telephone, and would precede large vessels in order to seek out obstructions and also clear the path for flying boats. *Good Hope Castle* was the first vessel to use what was termed 'blind pilotage', or navigating under the surveillance of port radar no matter what the weather. Commander Andrew, the Harbour Master at the time, foresaw the new system as the precursor to a whole array of such facilities wherever a ship might go. The Southampton experiment was in fact the catalyst for international agreement on the means of navigating ships safely into port at all times despite adverse weather conditions.

The London & South Western Railway established a private telephone exchange in the Docks in 1900. Initially this had an operator, who was housed in Dock House, and twelve lines. The exchange was later moved to the Marine and Wharfingers' Office, to which 140 lines were directed. In 1921 an automatic exchange was created with 300 lines. This meant that for the first time in any port, employees at Southampton who had a telephone in their office could dial each other without having to make their call through an operator. By 1930 the hub of the system, now with 400 lines, had moved again to premises near the Terminus Station for ease of connection to the railway 'trunk' system. The docks telephone system was a victim of enemy attack during the Second World War, but as communication with the outside world was essential, the Dock Telephone Exchange was reopened in a concrete bunker known as 'N' Vault in 1942. There was a manual exchange with three operators forming a link with the outside world and an automatic exchange connecting the internal network.

In 1950, Southampton became the first port in the country to provide telephone connections to ships when they berthed. On Sunday 9 November 1958 a new telephone exchange near Dock Gate 5 came into use. It still had a manual exchange for external calls, but the system was separated from the railway and had its own number for those telephoning from outside. Here, fifty lines were provided for the ship-to-shore service from a total of 600 lines that were available. The two master clocks regulating time throughout the Docks (one had been brought from 'N' Vault) were located in the new exchange, which itself had the new 'jumping numeral' – that is digital – clocks.

The modern Vessel Traffic Services building at Dock Head, as recommissioned in 2002. This is the site of the old Dock Head Signal Station. (Author)

Today we might think of using the Internet to access weather information but Southampton people used to contact the airport for this service. Growing public demand caused the Met Office and the Air Ministry to open Port Meteorological Offices. Southampton had the fourth such 'weather centre' in the country, the others being in London, Glasgow and Manchester. It opened in early January 1962 at 160 High Street and took much of its data not from satellite but from 'voluntary observations' from ships coming in to port. These vessels took measurements of the atmosphere and passed these on to the weather centre for analysis and for use in the preparation of weather forecasts.

Time and tide wait for nobody and in late 1968 a working party was established to consider new premises for the signal station at 37 Berth. The new facility would also unite the Trinity House pilots and the Harbour Master's department under one roof and enable the unmanned Calshot Signal Station to transmit its data by microwave. The scheme was approved and work started on the six-storey Port Communications Centre in late 1970. It was officially opened on 7 July 1972 by Mr R.F. Pugh, a representative of the British Transport Docks Board.

Data from the two remote radar scanners at Calshot and Hythe could now be used to give a more comprehensive picture of vessel movements. Vessel Traffic Services (VTS) was the name for this extended facility. Originally the scanner screens had to be viewed in a darkened room, but daylight screens were introduced, along with computer track-ing equipment, in 1989. A completely redesigned system incorporating four satellite radar scanners and closed-circuit television, together with a digital recording system that brings together dialogue from various sources, was introduced during 2001. The whole system is controlled electronically by a bespoke computerised traffic management system called PAVIS (Port and Vessel Information System). The new VTS was re-commissioned by the Princess Royal on 1 July 2002, taking its place at the forefront of new technology by adding AIS, an Automatic Identification System for ships, to its repertoire.

# COMPUTING

Mention has been made of the PAVIS traffic management program. Southampton has kept up to date with computer technology from the outset. It was one of ten ports linked to the BTDB computer centre in Southall, Middlesex, which became operational in the spring of 1969 and used an English Electric System 4-50 mainframe machine. Data was fed from terminals in ten ports, including Southampton, and was processed and returned, as was the way in those days, in printed form. The management felt that the computer would give a more rapid and comprehensive appreciation of the business activities of the port and book-keeping for Southampton was one of its first jobs. In September 1979 a new ICL 2960 mainframe computer was installed at Southall which was larger and faster, but still dealt only with accounting, statistics, payroll, pensions, stores and scientific research.

Not long after privatisation, ABP set up ABP Computer Services Ltd (ABPCS). Sixteen ports were now linked directly to the mainframe. In September 1987 this machine was again upgraded to an ICL 3960 and the ports acquired ICL minicomputers for spread-sheets and word processing, and in order to access the mainframe machine via telephone lines. There were difficulties of compatibility with IBM machines, so ABPCS helped make software available for business applications. Specialised local applications were developed, including Trident, an early traffic management system that monitored the movement of vessels and hazardous goods which was specially developed for Southampton.

Independent of the systems being put in place at the port, Community Network Services Ltd (CNS) was set up in 1987 as a subsidiary of Southampton Container Terminal. The company, which had its headquarters in Fareham, developed Direct Trader Input to provide critical information on the movement of goods and to enable speedy clearance through customs. In Southampton this was also linked to the port operational systems showing vessel movements and tracking of cargo. Today CNS belongs to DP World and is based in the Container Port. It is the UK's leading provider of electronic data interchange, enabling the freight industry to transfer information efficiently and get goods through customs, not just in Southampton but in other parts of the country. It therefore has a major impact on the worldwide flow of cargo from producers to final customers. In the late 1990s it developed SPIN, the Southampton Port Information Network, integrating such things as customs clearance, delivery instructions, manifests, ship planning, container tracking and hazard information, and keeping such bodies as Trading Standards and Port Health informed.

Let us consider for a moment why this overwhelming dependence on electronics is so important. The citizen can be assured that nothing is smuggled, that the appropriate dues have been paid and that lorries bringing containers to and from the Docks are scheduled to cause minimum congestion. The consumer can be assured that the product they seek is in the right place at the right time and that foodstuffs are wholesome. The driver of a straddle carrier will move the correct box to the correct stack and place it in the correct sequence in order that it goes not only on the correct ship, but in a sequence that allows it to be unloaded at its destination without fuss and in a way that maintains the stability of the ship.

3

# THE HUMAN CONNECTION

## MAIL

In earlier times communication with people in other countries had to be by letter, unless one went in person, and these letters had to be carried by sea. The Admiralty initially controlled the carriage of mail using swift sailing cutters. Operations from Southampton began in 1781, sailing fortnightly to the Channel Islands with goods and passengers as well as the mail.

With the coming of the steamship, the government solicited tenders from private companies to take on the responsibility for communication with countries overseas. The successful bidder would be awarded an exclusive contract to carry the mail for a specific period provided they met certain requirements, including speed and regularity of service. Cunard won one of these early contracts in 1840, but this did not involve the use of vessels sailing out of Southampton.

Businesses who were awarded the mail contracts were paid quite handsomely by the government to carry out their duties. When the recently formed Union Steamship Co. won the contract to convey mail to South Africa they were awarded £30,000 a year for a monthly sailing to and from Cape Town. The subvention, or subsidy, from the government amounted to £1,250 per voyage, which should be contrasted with an average income of £855 per trip from the conveyance of goods and passengers. The three-masted schooner-rigged steamship *Dane* inaugurated this service from Southampton on 15 September 1857, carrying only six passengers. In 1876 the renewed mail contract was shared jointly by the Union Line and the Castle Line, and for the first three years there was an additional incentive payment of £150 for every day that the mail reached its destination ahead of the contracted time, although this payment was later greatly reduced. Mail contracts were therefore a great stimulus to the foundation and maintenance of trade routes, and also encouraged improvements in the design of steamships.

In Southampton, the Union Line had been preceded by two other steamship companies operating mail services. P&O operated a monthly mail service to Alexandria from 1840 with the *Oriental*. In the early days of the service the vessel had to leave from the Royal Pier, as the commercial docks were not then in operation. Another pioneering company, the Royal Mail Steam Packet Co., was engaged on two routes for the delivery of overseas mail; the first to the West Indies, commencing with the *Forth* in December 1841, and the second to Brazil and the River Plate. This last mentioned service was officially inaugurated by the *Teviot* on 9 June 1851, but the *Esk* had already made an experimental voyage to Rio de Janeiro and Buenos Aires toward the end of 1850.

The building at 57 High Street, which was the P&O offices in 1845, later become the Head Post Office and a separate Docks Post Office was built in 1909. This later became the GPO Telex Centre and has more recently been converted into apartments.

Southampton became one of the major postal offices in the country and a principal port for the exchange of foreign mails, not only because it handled all the post for a large city and a considerable area surrounding it, but because it was conveniently placed to send and receive mail from many foreign countries. In the twentieth century it became the centre for sorting, bagging and despatching surface mail going to the United States and to central and South Africa, a role it eventually came to undertake for the entire country outside London.

Little changed until mail handling processes were mechanised and Southampton again led the way in the introduction of new technology. The prototypes of the automatic letter facer, a machine for turning letters the right way up with the stamp in the top right-hand corner, and the single-position letter sorting machine were tested here in

December 1957 and July 1958 respectively before going into general use throughout the country. Southampton was allocated postcodes in 1967, partly to assist further with mechanisation, before the system was extended to cover almost the whole country by 1973.

The Post Office in Southampton had been using containers to send mail to and from the USA since 1969, and the Far East and Channel Islands since 1972. The connection with the old mail service to South Africa was finally broken on 27 October 1977, when the Union Castle ship *Southampton Castle* brought the last consignment of what was then considered conventional mail in bags. Her Master, Captain Wray, handed a symbolic letter from the Mayor of Cape Town to Councillor Joyce Pitter, the Mayor of Southampton, to mark the occasion. Some five weeks later the container ship *Table Bay* docked, heralding the new system for conveying mail from overseas.

These containers, along with foreign mail coming from ships and the mail gathered from Southampton and its hinterland, were taken to the Western Dock Sorting Office near Dock Gate 10, which had been opened by the Postmaster General in May 1966. An adjoining site of 2 acres (0.8 hectares) was acquired for the construction of a Parcel Concentration Office, which started work on New Year's Day 1973. This too was a prototype of mechanisation and was the first of twenty-seven such depots throughout the country. Mail received from ships was brought in rail vehicles to an unloading platform at the office and mail for shipment was returned in the same vans. Initially, mail going long distances inland was despatched in rail vehicles from another platform, but a change to the use of road transport occurred well before the office closed in 2008.

It was noted in 1958 that 'much first-class mail goes by air', but the volume of surface mail continued to increase so that in the 1960s, over 1.6 million bags were sent from or received into the Docks. The *Queen Elizabeth* would typically take 5,000 bags to or from the United States and, in a busy week, up to 50,000 bags could be handled. The stock of half a million post bags for overseas mail for the entire country was cleaned and stored in a depot in Redbridge.

## TENDERS

Due to increased passenger traffic and the greater number of ships coming to use the port, some vessels had to anchor at Cowes Roads, off East Cowes, and transfer passengers, luggage, stores and mail by means of a tender, a vessel designed to convey them from ship to land. A facility for the receipt and despatch of tenders was opened on 20 July 1914. This Tender Station had a refreshment room for passengers, with catering provided by Spiers & Pond. Unfortunately only five ships were handled, one belonging to Union Castle and two each from Hamburg America Line and the German East Africa Line, before war broke out and the station closed, not to reopen until June 1925. The German East Africa Line returned, but from December 1926 decided to bring its ships in to dock rather than to use tenders. Less than a year later, United States Lines stopped using tenders when the *George Washington* docked. Norddeutscher Lloyd, which had used tenders for its Atlantic service since the nineteenth century, abandoned the practice when it brought the *Bremen* into the New Docks in May 1933. French Line ships had always been met by tenders in order to avoid the delay caused to their Atlantic services by actually coming into Southampton, but in November 1937 they too followed suit and brought *Champlain* in to dock at the port, although *Normandie* continued to be tendered until the outbreak of the Second World War.

Despite these changes to the way passengers and goods were brought to the quayside, the towing companies continued to maintain an impressive tender fleet. In the 1920s the Alexandra Towing Co., which had come to Southampton when Cunard moved its express service in 1919, employed two tenders, the *Flying Kestrel* and *Romsey*, while the Southampton, Isle of Wight & South of England Royal Mail Steam Packet Co. (which later adopted the name Red Funnel and a new livery for convenience), had no less than seven saloon paddle steamers at its disposal when required and two tug tenders, *Albert Edward* and *Vulcan*. In 1930, these were joined by the tug tender *Calshot*.

Tenders were once again in demand when passenger services resumed in the years following the Second World War. Passengers were landed by tender at the new Ocean Terminal as soon as it became available and also at the Western Docks, and the tug companies brought in new vessels to carry on this trade. Red Funnel introduced the 400-passenger *Gatcombe* to replace *Paladin* in 1960 and the Alexandra Towing Co. replaced the ageing *Romsey* with *Flying Breeze* in 1962. Red Funnel acquired *Calshot (II)* to replace *Calshot* in March 1964. French Line reverted to the old way of handling passengers and mail by tender and the first job for *Gatcombe* was to receive passengers from *Liberté* on 8 July 1960. French Line continued the use of tenders until *France* docked on her inaugural cruise to the Canaries on 20 January 1962, and thereafter the use of tenders declined.

## RISE OF NORTH ATLANTIC TRADE

There had been some tentative attempts to operate steamships between Southampton and the United States from the start of commercial docks in what was still an era of experimentation. The Belgian government acquired the *British Queen* in 1842, but she only made three crossings from Antwerp to New York, via Southampton, before being broken up. The Ocean Steam Navigation Co. operated its two ships between Bremen, Southampton and New York for ten years before being wound up in 1857. The New York & Havre Steam Navigation Co. placed its first ship on this route via Southampton in 1850, and was joined by the *Vanderbilt* of Vanderbilt Line on the same transatlantic route in 1857. While the New York & Havre Steam Navigation Co. lost two of its ships early on, it continued, along with the Vanderbilt Line, until late in 1861 when the American Civil War, having broken out in April, put pay to these services.

According to a paper produced by the Institute of Naval Architects, Hamburg America Line and Norddeutscher Lloyd, which began using Southampton in 1857 and 1858 respectively, were enterprising pioneers that gradually drew much of the ocean passenger traffic from the north of England to the south. Bremen, the home port of Norddeutscher Lloyd, had had a commercial treaty with the United States since 1828. Perhaps influenced by these activities, the move of American Line from Liverpool to Southampton in March 1893 was said to be prompted by the proximity of continental Europe; the more convenient links to London, which was 100 miles (161km) closer by rail; the sheltered deep-water harbour; and the presence of better dock facilities. The coming of American Line was therefore recognised from the outset as being highly significant in the development of Southampton.

The Mayor and Corporation went out to meet the first of the American Line ships, the *New York*, on-board the London & South Western Railway paddle steamer *Wolf*, which was dressed all over for the occasion. The *New York* was escorted up Southampton Water and into the port, and her first passengers were met by a train, the *American Eagle*, which con-

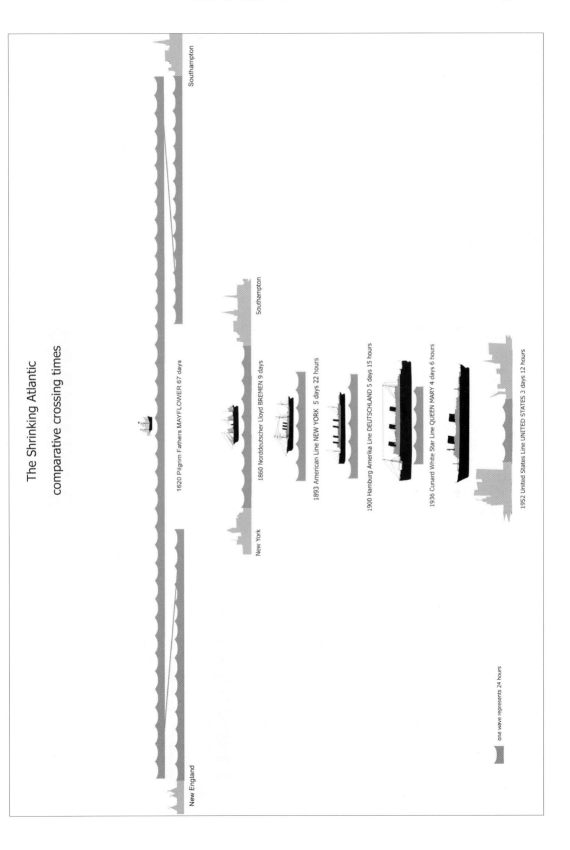

The Shrinking Atlantic
comparative crossing times

Southampton

1620 Pilgrim Fathers MAYFLOWER 67 days

Southampton

1860 Norddeutscher Lloyd BREMEN 9 days

1893 American Line NEW YORK 5 days 22 hours

1900 Hamburg Amerika Line DEUTSCHLAND 5 days 15 hours

1936 Cunard White Star Line QUEEN MARY 4 days 6 hours

1952 United States Line UNITED STATES 3 days 12 hours

New York

New England

one wave represents 24 hours

veyed them to London. There then followed a week of shipping and civic celebrations. The public was admitted to view the *New York* for 1*s* (5p) a head. Over 3,000 visited the ship and the proceeds were given to charity. The *New York* and her sister *Paris* were the largest ships in the world at the time – if one discounts the unsuccessful *Great Eastern* – and at 10,508 tons were more than twice the size of the next biggest ship then to use Southampton, the *Mexican* of Union Line. The *New York* and *Paris* established new standards in luxury and speed on the North Atlantic and their presence promoted feeder services such as those operated by the General Steam Navigation Co. These standards were maintained by subsequent ships of the line, such as the *St Louis* of 1895.

The original offices of American Line were in Canute Chambers in Canute Road, later celebrated as the home of White Star Line. When White Star moved to Southampton in 1907, *Adriatic* was the company's first ship to call. She was then the largest ship using the Docks and was met on her arrival from New York on 29 May by a civic party in a railway paddle steamer, and led into the Docks. There was less visible jubilation than had been shown on the arrival of American Line, but the position of Southampton was strengthened by the arrival of the White Star Co. to the port. White Star's decision to move its express transatlantic service from Liverpool had been taken with a view to securing a share of the Continental passenger trade, and the company ships soon began to call at Cherbourg. So successful was White Star in gaining the cross-Channel traffic that a decision was soon made to double the size of its ships. This decision had an impact on the facilities that had to be provided at the port and a new deep-water dock, initially called White Star Dock, was provided, from which the *Olympic* departed on her maiden voyage on 14 June 1911. She was the first of three proposed super liners and the largest British-built ship at 46,439 tons until the arrival of the *Queen Mary*. The second of those ships, the *Titanic*, departed from the same berth on 10 April 1912, but sank on her maiden voyage with great loss of life. The third vessel, *Britannic*, which never entered passenger service, was lost during the First World War.

White Star Dock was renamed Ocean Dock in 1922 and the following year *Majestic* of 56,551 tons joined the White Star fleet. This was the former German liner *Bismarck* and had been assigned to White Star under the reparations scheme. In 1928 Cunard and United States Lines, which had taken over from American Line in 1921, jointly introduced improved provision for 'cabin passengers and tourist third cabin travellers'. The following year Cunard announced 'Atlantic holidays from £38 return' in order to maintain its position in a difficult market during a period of great economic uncertainty. During the early part of 1932, Cunard and White Star arranged to operate alternate weekly sailings across the Atlantic and in May there were 'substantial reductions in fares' to try to attract custom, with the companies reverting to alternate sailings in October. Finally, in May 1934, Cunard merged with White Star to form Cunard White Star Ltd In December 1949, the name of the company changed again, to the Cunard Steam Ship Co. This reversion to the Cunard name took many years to be completed, and the author remembers seeing a 'Cunard White Star' gangway in use with the *Queen Mary* in 1960.

Cunard has had longer associations with Southampton than many people suspect. Its ships, *Aurania*, *Catalonia* and *Servia*, initially came to the port as transport ships, bearing numbers 20, 21 and 31, during the Boer War. In 1911 the company transferred its Canadian service to Montreal and Quebec from London to Southampton. Cunard's rivals on the route, Canadian Pacific, had started its Canadian service from Southampton in August 1910, although its express service did not start until after the First World War.

*Left:* Canute Chambers, the offices of American Line from 1893 and later of White Star Line. The building is shown as it appeared after the Second World War when it housed the Netherlands Consulate. The large windows on the ground floor were originally subdivided into three parts. (Author)

*Below:* The passenger and cargo shed at Ocean Dock under construction in 1911. This remained in use until it was badly damaged during the Second World War. It was subsequently replaced by the Ocean Terminal. (Author)

Cunard's express service to New York was inaugurated on 14 June 1919 when *Aquitania* sailed with 5,000 Canadian troops. The passenger and cargo sheds at 43 Berth and 44 Berth had been completed in January and September 1912, but after war service they were released by the government only in 1919 and therefore could not be occupied sooner by Cunard.

Gradually, trade began to flow once more through the port. Old services were revived after the Armistice and new ones were established by shipping companies that had become aware of Southampton's advantages as a port. Orient Line's seasonal service to Australia started in 1926, the same year that the Cunard London to New York ships started calling at Southampton. In April 1937, Cunard started making some of its liners available for public inspection, and the *Berengaria* was opened for three days the same month. The Second World War brought a temporary end to most civilian passenger traffic. The first fare-paying passengers to cross the Atlantic from Southampton to New York after the Second World War were carried on the Swedish-America Line *Gripsholm* in March 1946.

After the Second World War, Cunard started a gradual withdrawal of services from its former home port of Liverpool. There had been an office in the Docks at Southampton for many years and this, having been destroyed during the war, was replaced in 1954 by a new building near 46 Berth known as Trafalgar Chambers. The company's Baggage Store was opened in Harcourt Road in 1951 and its bonded warehouses followed in 1962. By March 1966, the Freight Department had been established in Canute Road and the offices of the Catering, Purchasing, Shops and Lady Superintendent's Departments were already installed in what became the main offices in South Western House. This building was the former South Western Hotel, which had never reverted to its original purpose after being requisitioned by the Navy in 1940.

Engraving by Newman of the South Western Hotel. The building was built as the Imperial Hotel in 1867 and was renamed in 1870 before being taken over by the railway. A large extension was built in 1882. (Private collection)

Bennett's Refreshment Rooms at 34 Berth. This was the second such establishment to be opened in the Docks, the first being at 30 Berth. The building was removed in the late 1920s. (Author)

There was a revival of Cunard Line Open Days on 4 April 1966 when 1,200 people came to see *Queen Mary*, and there were a further twenty-seven Open Days in the period until October that year, when the public could see what life was like on-board the company's ships. The transfer from Liverpool was formally completed when the first meeting of the directors took place in Southampton on 18 July 1966.

When Southampton was Britain's 'Premier Ocean Passenger Port', there were certain trends in passenger traffic that could be relied upon. There was a period in the depths of winter when crossing the Atlantic was undesirable because of bad weather, but although the passenger season opened in March it didn't peak until June, when the numbers travelling from west to east were sometimes called the 'American invasion'. August brought a surge in numbers in the other direction, from east to west, back across the Atlantic.

## ACCOMMODATION

A glance at any detailed dock map prior to the Second World War would have shown the quayside more or less completely built up with sheds which were almost all identified as 'cargo and passenger shed'. In other words, the two functions were indistinguishable and the nature of the activities depended only on the kind of vessel moored alongside. Different companies had their own preferred locations on the quayside and there were canteens sited in various places where passengers' needs could be catered for

In 1931 a new Ocean Restaurant was built at 45 Berth, although this was demoted to serving snacks after the opening of Ocean Terminal in 1950. Other catering facilities for passengers were operated first by Spiers & Pond Ltd, and then Frederick Hotels Ltd until the Docks were nationalised in 1948. These facilities then became part of the British Transport Commission's Hotel and Catering Services and were provided in the waiting hall at 102 Berth, and at 105 and 107 Sheds.

The firm perhaps best known for its catering facilities is Bennett's (Southampton) Ltd
W.E. Bennett set up his business in the Docks in 1886, serving passengers from trestle
tables on the quayside. His first permanent canteen was intended for both passengers and
port employees and, as such, was the first of its kind in Britain. In later years, Bennett's
catered only for Dock employees.

Passengers in the early years of the twentieth century were landed at or departed
from surroundings that were, at best, unremarkable. The destruction that took place
during the Blitz now presented a splendid opportunity for the provision of facilities of
an entirely new order. In May 1946 an inspection party stood on the broken floor of the
former White Star passenger shed at 44 Berth, which had been rendered unserviceable by
enemy action. The party included the Southern Railway's General Manager, Sir Eustace
Missenden, and Docks and Marine Manager Mr R.P. Biddle, and they were discussing
plans for building a modern Ocean Terminal, with everything for the passenger under
one roof, presented in the most favourable conditions.

Much research had been undertaken overseas, particularly in the United States, Canada
and Europe, to find all the latest and most innovative trends in passenger handling. The
Chairman of the Southern Railway and his fellow directors thought it highly advanta-
geous to go ahead with the proposal that was put to them and for which they obtained
the support of the Minister of Transport. This was seen as a project of national prestige,
with the potential to act as a model for all other passenger accommodation ashore. After
the Docks were nationalised in 1948, the Railway Executive remained committed to the
plan and pursued it energetically.

The building, which was designed by Mr C.B. Dromgoole, the architect in the Chief
Docks Engineer's Department, was to be of pre-cast concrete and 395m (nearly a quarter of
a mile) long. The semi-circular tower at one end was not only a landmark, but was initially
home to Customs and the bonded baggage store. In order to ensure that such a long, thin
building was attractive as well as functional, the opinion of the Fine Art Commission was
sought. The resulting structure allowed passengers to arrive by train and be conveyed by
escalator to the first floor, where they could wait in air-conditioned comfort and have their
needs catered for, safe from the bustle of docks activities beneath. They then joined their ship
via telescopic light alloy gangways, the first of their kind, which linked directly with the ship
and folded up against the building when not in use. Access for visitors or those saying good-
bye to passengers was via a pre-stressed concrete bridge over the railway to a balcony on the
quayside. The building was constructed by Staverton Builders Ltd of Totnes, with interior
decoration and furnishings by Maple & Co. Ltd of London. Facilities were duplicated, for
first and cabin class passengers remained separate. Both reception halls, for instance, had their
own book stall provided by W.H. Smith & Son, a company that had obtained its first contract to sell books and newspapers in Southampton Docks on 1 April 1852.

For the official opening on 31 July 1950 the Prime Minister, Clement Attlee, arrived
from London at the platform beneath the new building on 'No.1 Ocean Terminal
Express', pulled by the locomotive *Channel Packet*. *Queen Elizabeth* was the first ship to
depart from the Ocean Terminal, twenty-four hours after the opening ceremony, and the
first inward ship to use the facilities was *Queen Mary* on 3 August 1950.

On Saturday 2 September, Ocean Terminal was opened for public inspection and 3,000
came. From its opening until the end of the year, forty-three liners and tenders, and 38,000
passengers used the new facility. While the building was in operation about 40 per cent
of ocean-going passengers at Southampton used Ocean Terminal. From 1952 the famous

NEW PASSENGER TERMINAL-OCEAN DOCK-SOUTHAMPTON

**STAVERTON   BUILDERS   LIMITED**

CONTRACTORS

TOTNES · SOUTH DEVON

———————— TELEPHONES ————————

Totnes   2252 - 4   —   VICtoria  0800   —   Southampton   4928

*Above left:* A pre-war view of *Queen Mary* alongside the
White Star terminal at Ocean Dock. The building in front of the terminal is the passenger refreshment
rooms. (Stan Roberts)

*Above right:* Builder's advertisement featuring the Ocean Terminal (Private Collection)

Dock Model of 1939 was displayed in the South Tower, as it had become known, and from
late 1955 the BBC had use of a room in which to interview 'prominent people' as they
passed through the port.

The original Ocean Terminal remained in operation for thirty-three years. It may have
been the grandest passenger terminal at the time, but it was not the last. The first piles for
a new cargo and incoming passenger terminal to replace the existing shed at 102 Berth
were driven in October 1952 and the completed building, designed by the Docks Engineer
J.H. Jellett, was opened by the High Commissioner for South Africa, His Excellency
Mr G.P. Jooste, on 25 January 1956. The new building was intended for the use of Union
Castle mail steamers, and the first ship to dock alongside was the *Edinburgh Castle* on 10
February 1956. This site was later redeveloped as part of the Free Trade Zone. Another
passenger terminal was created at 105-106 Berth specifically for the P&O ships *Canberra*
and *Oriana*, which were to be based in and operated from Southampton. This building was
opened by Field Marshal Sir William Slim, the former Governor General of Australia, in
November 1960. It featured an abstract mural by R.A. Sullock and R.D. King as one of its
attractions. While extensively modified and updated, this remains a cruise terminal today.

In October 1963, Ministry of Transport approval was sought for the construction of
another new passenger terminal at 38-39 Berth. The consultant engineers for this project
were Gifford & Partners and the architect Ronald Sims was responsible for the interior
treatment. This building was opened by Her Majesty the Queen, accompanied by the
Duke of Edinburgh, on 15 July 1966 and approval to call the building the Queen Elizabeth
II Terminal was granted in February 1967. The first ship to use it was the P&O Orient Line
*Iberia* arriving from the Far East on 1 October 1966. New furnishings, carpets and a public
address system were installed in 1988 and in April 1995 a major restructuring of the vehicle
and passenger flow took place; the passenger lounge was extended, another visitor waiting
area was added and the customs, immigration and security facilities were upgraded. Its most
recent remodelling was completed in 2003, when it was reopened by Mrs Pauline Prescott,
wife of the then Deputy Prime Minister.

A new passenger ferry terminal was constructed at 2 Berth in Outer Dock. This dock was renamed Princess Alexandra Dock on 3 July 1967 when the new terminal was opened by Her Royal Highness Princess Alexandra, the Hon. Mrs Angus Ogilvy. The main structure consisted of twelve curved and laminated timber arches made by the local firm of Gabriel, Wade & English. The ends of this 167ft long building were glazed, allowing passengers, especially those standing on the mezzanine level, to see the activity taking place at the ferry terminal. They may not have done so in comfort though, in spite of the under-floor heating, as a contemporary account of the building notes that, 'The transistorised public address system has equipment for continuous playing of tape-recorded music'. The building has since been demolished. Princess Alexandra Dock was idle when Associated British Ports took over the ownership of the Docks in 1983, the passenger ferry trade having ceased. The *Financial Times* summed up the position very well in 1986 by stating ABP had been 'freed from the legislative straitjacket which consigned countless acres of unwanted dockland to continuing dereliction'. The company was not slow in developing the potential of some of these assets. It had already planned a comprehensive redevelopment of the area in 1985 and began its first and largest regeneration project, focusing on that part of the Eastern Docks considered no longer suitable for modern shipping needs, to form Ocean Village. The Harbour Lights cinema now stands on the site of the former terminal within Ocean Village. The Town Quay redevelopment project followed under Bargate Securities in 1987. These two waterfront developments were re-branded in an innovative public/private sector initiative with Southampton City Council. The partnership scheme was called 'Waterfront Southampton', and was launched in the spring of 1990.

The P&O Terminal at 106 Berth was modernised in 1987 and was given a major refurbishment in April 1992 when it was renamed the Mayflower Terminal. As this is its home berth, P&O Cruises played an integral part in its refurbishment, modernising the passenger lounge and adding new reception, check-in and baggage-handling facilities. A new ramped and covered overhead gangway system was also introduced. It was brought up to date again in 2007 by the Winchester architectural practice of Househam Henderson. P&O Princess Cruises became part of the Carnival Corporation, which also has Cunard and Holland America Line among its brands, in April 2003.

The original passenger lounge of the Queen Elizabeth II Terminal at 38-39 Berths. (Associated British Ports)

The City Cruise Terminal was created from the old Windward fruit terminal and opened in August 2003. Expansion of the cruise business caused it to be extended and upgraded in 2005. When the remodelled terminal reopened in April 2007, the first ship to use the facility was the *Navigator of the Seas* belonging to Royal Caribbean International.

Most recently the name 'Ocean Terminal' has been revived by the construction of a new building of this name at 46 and 47 Berths in the Ocean Dock, opposite the place where the original Ocean Terminal once stood. This was opened on 9 May 2009 by the Port Director, Doug Morrison, and the Chief Executive of Carnival UK, David Dingle, when the *Ventura* was the first vessel officially to depart. Unofficially, the P&O cruise ship *Oceana* had called at the berth the week before. This terminal, though modern in concept, follows many of the ideas pioneered by its predecessor, and all four current passenger terminals now have high-level gangways to the ships. They are used today almost exclusively by cruise ships and, as the ABP Marketing Manager Patrick Bowyer observed in 1997, 'It is time for the shore side to enter the new age of cruising. Cruising is a five-star experience, after all. Terminals must match the ship in terms of standard and facilities as far as possible'.

## REVIVAL AND DECLINE OF CONVENTIONAL PASSENGER SERVICES

P&O returned to Southampton in 1925 with the first sailing of its Far Eastern service marked by the departure of the *Khyber* on 4 July. On 29 April 1929 the *Bangalore* inaugurated a new service to India, and the company's cruise ships also returned to Southampton the same year. Passenger and cargo services to India and the Far East were suspended during the Second World War but resumed after the conflict.

In 1960 a new P&O Orient Line vessel, *Oriana*, was based in Southampton, followed by *Canberra* in 1961, two of the largest and fastest ships built in the country since the *Queen Mary* and *Queen Elizabeth*. The other seven P&O passenger ships plying between London and Australia also moved to Southampton in the summer to operate as cruise ships. From October 1969 P&O concentrated all its passenger operations in Southampton, its ships continuing their Australian services from the port in the season from March to June and then cruising for the rest of the year.

P&O had had a stake in Orient Line since the end of the First World War, but the companies continued to operate separately until P&O-Orient Lines Passenger Services Ltd and a similarly named management company were formed in 1960. From 1 October 1966 the entire enterprise was known simply as P&O.

At the end of 1969 the company announced that it would stop calling at Indian ports, a route that the company had operated from early in its history. It is said that the word 'posh' was coined in Southampton, as the most expensive tickets on the Indian route were stamped with the letters POSH, or 'Port Out, Starboard Home'. Anyone holding one of these tickets had to be given a portside cabin on the voyage out and a starboard cabin coming home. Such cabins, which were always in the shade and caught the prevailing winds in hot climates, were seen as highly desirable and worth paying extra for.

Old ships reaching the end of their useful lives were not an unusual site in Southampton. Cunard's *Aquitania*, the last of the 'big six' liners, was withdrawn from service at the end of 1949 and laid up at 109 Berth. Her demise was remarkable because of the week-long sale of her fittings at the quayside by Hampton's in April 1950. The *Britannic* retired at the end of 1960. In the summer of 1964, Nederland Line stopped operating passenger services.

The offices of Carnival UK at 100 Harbour Parade, Southampton. (Author)

Operations across the North Atlantic were also undergoing a period of change. *Queen Mary* returned from her farewell cruise on 19 October 1967 before departing for California and *Queen Elizabeth* did likewise on 15 November 1968. Royal Mail Line ceased passenger operations in early 1969 when *Amazon*, *Aragon* and *Arlanza* were withdrawn. Then at the end of 1969, the *United States*, a relatively new vessel, was withdrawn from the Atlantic route. No longer could one 'take the *United States* to America', as the advertisements said. And in 1971 Holland America Line, a company that had first come to Southampton in 1923, ended her Atlantic crossings in order to concentrate on cruising. The *France*, the flagship of French Line, was withdrawn at the end of 1974 having started regular crossings of the Atlantic only on 3 February 1962. On other routes, both the Fyffes Group and Royal Netherlands Steamship Co. stopped taking passengers to the West Indies in 1972. The P&O passenger ships that had been transferred from London were sold or broken up, beginning with the *Iberia* in 1972 and finishing with the withdrawal of the *Oronsay* in 1975. The Shaw, Savill & Albion ships *Ocean Monarch* and *Northern Star* made their last voyages in 1975.

There had been a big slump affecting passenger traffic on the North Atlantic that had begun in around 1930. At the time, Southampton fared better than other ports. There was only a 7.6 per cent reduction in passengers carried on this route, whereas nationally the reduction in passenger traffic was said to be as high as 44 per cent. Recovery was slow, but by 1937 there had been a complete revival. It was thought that perhaps such things were cyclical, and the companies comprising the Atlantic Passenger Steamship Conference seemed none too concerned when, in 1963, they carried 24,000 fewer passengers across the Atlantic, a drop of 3 per cent on the previous year. Their lack of concern seems principally to have been because the members had more than made up for this decline with cruise passengers.

The reason for the fall in passenger numbers was mentioned only briefly in the *Shipping Guide* as early as January 1959: 'On ocean routes, carryings [of passengers] by air have for the first time surpassed those by sea'. The industry still seemed to be unconcerned. In 1966, in spite of increasing competition from airlines, it was said that 'there is still a great future for sea travel'. And in 1969, 'liners on the North Atlantic route between Southampton and New York are still carrying very big complements', in spite of intense competition.

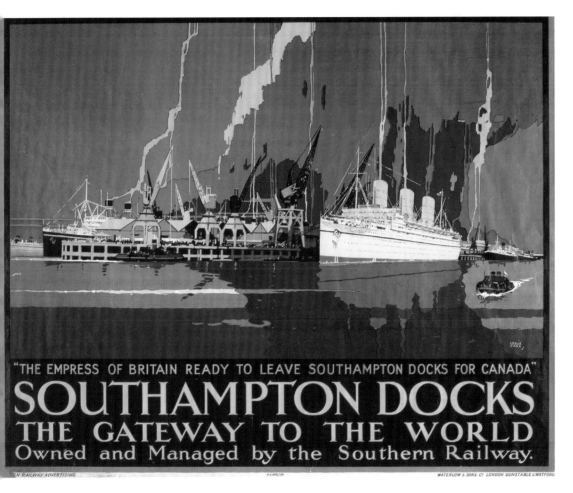

16  Lesley Carr's poster for the Southern Railway depicting a bustling scene at the Eastern Docks with the *Empress of Canada* of Canadian Pacific ready to depart. The poster is thought to have been issued in 1936, although the ship generally used the Western Docks which had been completed a few years before. (Southampton City Council, Arts and Heritage Services)

14 Following the opening of the new Ocean Terminal by David Dingle, CEO of Carnival UK, and Doug Morrison, Port Director of ABP, on 29 May 2009, an invited audience celebrates the departure of the P&C *Ventura*. (Carnival PLC)

15 Exterior of the new Ocean Terminal on opening day. (Carnival PLC)

*Above:* 12  Research ship *James Cook* in the Empress Dock outside the National Oceanography Centre. (National Oceanography Centre, Southampton University)

*Left:* 13  The new super post-Panamax Portainer cranes at 206 Berth in the Container Port. These reach out over a ship up to twenty-two containers wide and convey the container, or sometimes two together, to or from the quayside. They were built by Liebherr Container Cranes, partly in Germany and partly in Ireland, with the components being assembled on site and were first used on 14 June 2009 to discharge *CMA CGM Vela*. (DP World, Southampton)

*Left:* 10 The Container Port with the Redbridge Vehicle Terminal in the middle distance. Closer to the camera and towards the right-hand side of the photograph is the Maritime Rail Freight Terminal. Southampton is the UK's second largest container terminal. (DP World, Southampton)

*Below:* 11 The western end of the Container Port with the trees of Redbridge Wharf Park and the main Southampton to Poole railway line in the foreground. (Author)

7 Aerial view of the Western Docks taken in late 2009, with cruise ships at both the Mayflower and City Cruise Terminals. Container storage can also be seen on the old Post Office site. (Associated British Ports)

*Above left:* 8 The full extent of the Esso refinery at Fawley can only be seen from the air as at ground level it is substantially concealed by trees. Beyond the power station, in the top left-hand corner, is Calshot Spit. (ExxonMobil, Fawley)

*Above right:* 9 The mile-long Fawley Terminal looking towards the Eastern Docks. The very largest tankers often discharge part of their cargo of crude oil at Rotterdam to reduce the draught. This enables them to manoeuvre safely in the shallower waters of the Solent, where they berth at the jetties nearest the camera. (ExxonMobil, Fawley)

5 Colour photograph of Southampton Docks taken in September 1902. This very early and therefore extremely rare colour photograph shows the full extent of the Docks at the end of the Boer War. The cold store is the white concrete cube just to the right of the flagpole. (Giles Hudson)

6 The only survivor of five RAF-type Leyland buses of 1921, employed to take migrants to and from the transit camp at Atlantic Park. Many were poor people from Eastern Europe who, having arrived at Hull, were sent by train to Eastleigh to begin the next phase of their journey. The vehicle is owned and was restored superbly and accurately by Mr Stephen Hubbuck. (Author)

3  Print showing the crowds at the laying of the foundation stone marking the commencement of Southampton Docks on 12 October 1838. The stone is under the tripod just to the right of centre and beyond that it appears that the cannons on the Battery were fired to mark the occasion. (Southampton City Council, Arts and Heritage Services)

4  'View of Southampton 1855' by Frederick Lee Bridell. This picture was painted from Portswood, which was still very rural at that time, although the railway line can be seen beyond the figures in the foreground. Southampton was rapidly becoming industrialised and the smoke beyond Northam Bridge mainly emanates from the railway coke ovens. (Southampton City Council, Arts and Heritage Services)

1 Portrait of Joseph Liggins, the founding Chairman of the Southampton Dock Co., a post he held for forty years. (Associated British Ports)

2 Portrait of Admiral Sir Lucius Curtis, who laid the foundation stone inaugurating the Docks. The picture was painted after he became Provincial Grand Master for Hampshire in 1840. (Royal Gloucester Lodge)

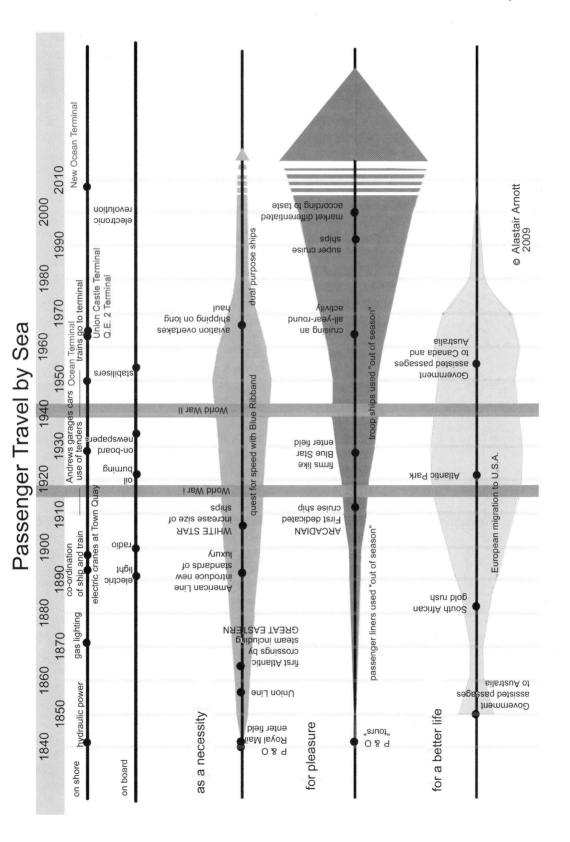

Passenger Travel by Sea

© Alastair Arnott
2009

There was a slight change of mood by 1971 when the *Shipping Guide* recorded, 'Despite a recession in ocean-going passenger traffic due principally to the withdrawal of the *United States* and a reduction in the number of trans-Atlantic voyages by vessels of the Holland-America Line, there have been several busy periods during the summer months'. Southampton had an ever-increasing share of what was a dwindling market, which is probably why the inevitable decline and its local impact were masked. In 1933, 36 per cent of passengers crossing the North Atlantic had done so from Southampton and by 1950 this had risen to 80 per cent. This tourist trade was one of the country's biggest dollar earners. At the same time, over 50 per cent of passengers going to and from South Africa passed through Southampton, which continued to increase its general hold on seaborne passenger traffic.

The Board of Trade statistics showing all the people entering and leaving the country on long sea voyages (that is excluding ferry crossings to the Continent or Ireland), showed that in 1926, 34 per cent of all passengers sailed from Southampton compared with 28 per cent leaving from or arriving at Liverpool. Excluding the period of the Second World War, there was an inexorable rise in the percentage leaving from Southampton so that by 1962 it had reached 62 per cent, whereas the percentage of passenger traffic using Liverpool had declined steadily to 15 per cent. The third big player in this was London which, in 1962, took 17 per cent of the trade, as usual within a few percentage points of the numbers recorded at Liverpool.

The perception of Southampton as the centre of the ocean liner trade has therefore been shown to be true. It took the lead from the late 1920s and between about 1950 and 1970 was the overwhelming leader, with four times the traffic of its nearest rival. Putting actual numbers to this is not so easy. There have always been some ferry passengers in addition to the deep sea ones. The Harbour Board, which was a separate entity, also handled large numbers of passengers from the Royal Pier. Then from the 1920s there were growing numbers of cruise passengers, not all of which were always segregated in the count. The Southern Railway souvenir guidebook that was published in 1930 gives a figure of 7,980 passengers using the Docks in 1824, although this is a misprint and the year referred to is actually 1842.

In 1892 there were said to be 122,108 recorded as having passed through Southampton, a number that had risen to 249,405 by 1914. After the First World War the figures probably also contain cruise passengers as well, but 1937 was a record year with 621,911. Following the Second World War, there were 587,357 passengers recorded in 1948. This number had risen to 780,902 by 1950, but had fallen back to about 500,000 by 1960. In the late 1960s and 1970s, with the coming of several ferry services, the numbers jump dramatically to 1.5 million. The only year for which there is an actual statistical breakdown of passenger numbers is 1969, when 484,217 ocean-going passengers were recorded as entering and leaving Southampton, and 675,573 cross-Channel passengers doing likewise.

Finally, in August 1977, *Docks* magazine described the passenger liner as 'fast becoming a vanished "breed"'. It was not, of course, completely extinct. *Queen Elizabeth 2* was, like the *Canberra*, intended to be a dual-purpose ship that could either cruise or operate on a regular passenger route. She made her first Atlantic crossing from Southampton on 17 January 1969 and her immediate popularity did much to stay the decline of this form of passenger travel. In her first season, much to the relief of her owners, Cunard, she performed even more successfully than expected, carrying 42,000 passengers on thirteen trips. She continued throughout her career to make some seasonal Atlantic crossings.

Paddle steamer *Solent Queen* at the Royal Pier. She was new to her owners, the Southampton, Isle of Wight & South of England Royal Mail Steam Packet Co. Ltd, in 1889 and continued in use with that company, apart from war service, until 1948. The photograph was taken after electric cranes were placed on the Town Quay in 1893 and before *Solent Queen* herself was fitted with electric light in 1907. (Brain collection)

In the face of increased competition, Ocean Travel Development was formed in 1958 by British passenger ship operators to promote their activities and stimulate interest, and Ocean Travel Fortnight was started that year to attract the public. This allowed potential customers to come and look at passenger ships participating in the event, which was usually held in November. It was slightly complicated by the necessity of visitors having to make an application through a travel agent. In 1966, 1,200 people came to Southampton from as far away as Wales and the Midlands to visit *Oriana,* which was one of only six ships participating that year. Ocean Travel Fortnight continued for a number of years until 1968. In 1976 the body running it became the Passenger Shipping Association, which still functions today with two main branches of membership, one for cruise operators and the other for ferry operators.

## MIGRATION

The Pilgrim Fathers are perhaps the best known group of migrants who set sail from Southampton in search of a better life overseas. In later years there was a government-assisted scheme to populate Australia in the 1840s and 1850s, and some of those people also sailed from Southampton. The departure of emigrant ships was one of the first uses of Inner Dock.

A major trend from the end of the nineteenth century had been the drift of people from Continental Europe seeking a better life in the New World of both North and South America. The transport of these passengers had been the raison d'être of some of the European shipping companies using Southampton and was also one of the reasons for the arrival of the White Star Line at the port. Some people came to Southampton from far afield and had to be accommodated prior to the departure of their ship, so a hostel, the Atlantic Hotel, was established for them. It was owned by John Doling and the foundation stone was laid in November 1893, although the building did not welcome its first visitor until the following year. The building still stands in Albert Road South, although it is now known as Atlantic Mansions and has been converted into residential apartments.

There is no record of how many people passed through this lodging house or any other, but in a five month period in 1905 no fewer than 37,285 people presented themselves to the US Consul in Southampton for inspection prior to emigration to the USA. The numbers of people wishing to emigrate became very large and, in 1923, a group of prominent shipping companies (Cunard, White Star and Canadian Pacific) established a holding centre at Atlantic Park, Eastleigh, where Southampton Airport now stands. The only reference to this in the whole fifty-three-year history of the *Shipping Guide* is in July 1926, when a reference is made to the 'modern hostel' provided at Eastleigh. However, the entry continues, 'A more recent development is the direct transhipment of emigrants from the continent at Southampton', which it was felt provided a quicker and better service.

The life of Atlantic Park, which more or less coincided with the government's Assisted Passage Scheme for British migrants going to Canada, ended in 1931. There was a further wave of migration from this country to Australia in the 1950s, 1960s and 1970s, for which the Australian government had ships on charter, *New Australia* of Shaw, Savill & Albion being a notable example. It replaced the *Georgic* with Sitmar's *Fairsea* in December 1955. In July 1970 Chandris Line won the Australian contract, although other companies also provided passage for emigrants. At the beginning of 1969 passenger traffic to Australia had been extremely heavy and within a three-day period, *Canberra* had sailed with 2,214, Chandris Line's *Ellinis* with 1,700 and Sitmar Line's *Castel Felice* with 1,340 people on-board. There were also migrants coming to this country from the West Indies, such as those arriving on the *Ascania* in 1955, although the numbers concerned were not nearly as great as the numbers leaving these shores.


## CRUISING

Sir Donald Anderson, speaking of the changing face of passenger shipping when Chairman of P&O in the 1960s, said, 'broadly, the passenger shipping companies are looking for their passenger support, not so much from people who have to travel by sea, as from those who wish to travel by sea'. This statement recognises the crucial shift in emphasis towards travelling for pleasure.

The first steamship companies in Southampton were engaged on mail contracts and therefore planned arrivals and departures from each port according to a published schedule. No enquiry was made as to a person's motivation for undertaking a voyage and no doubt some made such journeys for reasons other than business or government service. The idea of using empty space on scheduled services by attracting passengers who might not otherwise have travelled to these destinations occurred early to P&O. The company ran what were called 'tours' to Egypt and the Holy Land in the 1850s, employing writers like Thackeray to promote them. The Royal Mail Steam Packet Co. ran excursions to the Spithead Naval Reviews from August 1853, when the *Thames* carried passengers on a pleasure trip, which in this case also took in the Channel Islands and lasted two days. People with sufficient funds were also using the RMSP Co.'s transatlantic services to the West Indies to escape the winter weather in Britain. The company developed the idea further and, by the 1890s, had a well-established range of tours, where the passengers took a ship on a regular service to the Caribbean and transferred to a vessel of the inter-colonial mail service for a leisurely journey among the islands. The favoured option was the Special Tour of sixty-five days for £65, a considerable sum of money at the time.

The creation of the first dedicated cruise ship is credited to Albert Ballin of the Hamburg America Line. He persuaded his company to build *Prinzessin Victoria Luise* in 1901. She was a first-class-only ship, which made it unnecessary to duplicate facilities for different classes of passengers and meant that everyone on-board was entitled to use the full range of services and facilities on offer. She was also described as a 'cruising yacht'.

*Prinzessin Victoria Luise* never visited British ports, but the directors of the RMSP Co. were not far behind. In August 1904 they agreed to the *Solent* being used exclusively by tourists in the West Indies and borrowed Ballin's phrase by describing her as a 'cruising yacht'. She had the added attraction that, 'Her commander has discretion to vary the ports of call and the schedule of itinerary, in order that passengers' wishes may be considered wherever possible, and many interesting places are frequently visited, at which ordinary steamers do not call'. Passengers still had to travel out to the West Indies by scheduled steamer.

In the summer of 1908 *Amazon* sailed out and back to Norway with cruise passengers and immediately established the conventional cruise pattern where passengers complete a circular tour, returning to their home port on the same ship. The formula was so successful that the company converted one of its ships to be a dedicated cruise ship and the *Arcadian*, as she became, sailed for the first time on a cruise from Southampton in January 1912. Her destinations altered according to what was thought most suitable for the time of year, and so between June and August she sailed to Norwegian fjords and the Arctic. In September she went to the Mediterranean and in October to the Atlantic islands. A particular feature of the *Arcadian* was that she carried steam launches to take the passengers on excursions, which proved to be most useful when exploring otherwise inaccessible fjords.

The *Arcadian* did not survive the First World War, but her owners returned to the established pattern of cruising as soon as conditions allowed and added short tours to the Continent and to Madeira. A Great African Cruise was undertaken in 1926, departing from Southampton, and a similar venture lasting 101 days left port in January 1927. There were extensive winter cruises, although on a more modest scale, that took place until the outbreak of the Second World War, but RMSP Co. did not have the market to itself. Union Castle operated Christmas and New Year cruises and, by 1928, Cunard, Orient Line, Canadian Pacific and various Dutch companies, including Rotterdam Lloyd, which would take passengers to Java, had entered the field. Not to be outdone, Red Star were offering world cruises.

The boundaries between conventional sailings and cruises began to overlap as Cunard and United States Lines both announced improved provisions for Cabin and Tourist Third Class passengers in early 1928 in a move designed to encourage 'Atlantic holidays'. In 1929, Cunard advertised these 'Atlantic Holidays from £38 return'. In the same year Blue Star entered the cruise market with *Arandora Star*, a dedicated cruise ship based in Southampton, and P&O placed two of its 'Strath' cruise ships in Southampton. Canadian Pacific also undertook an annual four-month world cruise with *Empress of Britain*.

By 1933, nearly all the major shipping companies were engaged in cruising so that as other traffic decreased, it kept their ships in commission. Yeoward Line came to Southampton in 1933, Ellerman's City Line became regular visitors from 1934 and Lamport & Holt joined the mêlée in 1936. Aberdeen & Commonwealth Line was advertising round-voyage tickets to Australia, a total journey of ninety-seven days, for between £57 and £87 that year, but this was on their regular services. There were forty cruises departing from Southampton in 1927, which had risen to sixty by 1936 and eighty-five in 1937. This did not include weekend cruises to Normandy, Brittany and the Channel Islands, operated by the Southern Railway which had got in on the act using the ferry *St Briac*. By the late 1930s, cruising was one of the most popular forms of overseas holiday, although it remained beyond the means of most people.

After the Second World War, British Railways revived summer weekend cruises using the cross-Channel steamer *Falaise*, beating other British shipping companies by two years. The Norwegian *Venus* inaugurated 'Winter Sunshine' cruises to Madeira and Tenerife in the winter of 1948–49 and P&O returned in 1950, arranging six cruises to the Mediterranean and Portugal using the liners *Chusan* and *Himalaya*. That year the Bergen Steamship Co. brought back the *Stella Polaris* to Southampton, the ship having first come to the port in 1928. The revival of cruising was slow, owing to the disrupted conditions after the war and the non-availability of suitable ships. Nevertheless, in January 1953 the *Shipping Guide* was able to describe Southampton as 'again [being] the principal port for cruise ships'. There were twenty-seven summer cruises made from Southampton in 1956 and thirty in 1958. By 1968, there were ninety. British Railways expanded its cruise operations by bringing in the *Duke of Lancaster* from the London Midland Region to operate two six-day cruises to Holland, Belgium and France, and she continued these summer operations for a few years.

The 1960s were a period of expansion of the cruise industry, particularly in Southampton. While they were also years of restriction in the amount of money that could be taken abroad, expenses incurred while travelling on-board a British ship did not count and therefore one's meagre allowance could be spent on trips from the ship when in foreign ports. People were beginning to realise, perhaps because of the efforts of the industry itself, that cruising was not uniquely the preserve of the old and the wealthy. In fact, with growing leisure time and increased disposable income, many people were seeing the cruise as an alternative to the package holiday. The *Andes* of Royal Mail had sandwiched cruises between regular sailings to South America from May 1955 and was converted into a full-time single-class cruise ship (first class) in 1959. She continued in this role until the company's passenger services ceased in 1971, a victim of intense competition.

Union Castle had been a reluctant player in the cruise business, but placed *Warwick Castle* on cruising in January 1952, visiting South African ports and intermediate places such as Madeira. The company chartered its first dedicated cruise ship, *Reina Del Mar*, in 1964. The charter was renewed in 1968 and the ship continued to make between thirteen and fifteen cruises a year from Southampton. She was purchased outright by Union Castle in 1973, when the company had considered, but decided against, ordering a new cruise ship. *Reina Del Mar* was withdrawn from service on 1 April 1975 and regular liner services by Union Castle came to an end on 15 October 1977.

A nostalgic link was maintained by an annual cruise call made by the last White Star liner, the motor ship *Britannic*, although the connection ceased when she made her last voyage from Liverpool in November 1960. In spite of the emergence of the cruise ship as a specialist design several decades before, owners continued to divert liners to this traffic out of season. Thus the P&O ships were diverted from their regular London to Australia service to cruise from Southampton in the summer, a practice that continued until they were permanently transferred to Southampton in the autumn of 1969. P&O's *Oriana* and *Canberra* had already been based in Southampton since entering service, and both *Canberra* and *Queen Elizabeth 2* of Cunard had been designed to operate in the role of both cruise ship and ocean liner.

In the 1930s, British India Line had first employed its troop ships to perform educational cruises for schools during the summer months when not engaged in the transportation of military personnel. These educational cruises resumed in 1961 with *Dunera*. Moving troops by sea in peacetime ended in 1962, but the educational use continued. *Dunera* was later replaced by *Nevasa*, a vessel that continued in this role until withdrawn at the end of 1974. *Uganda* joined the fleet, making her first educational cruise to the Mediterranean on 27 February 1968, but she was different. *Uganda* was the first passenger ship to be adapted to this role, heralding a new era of relative comfort for her young passengers compared to that offered by ships that normally carried members of the armed forces.

It has long been the practice for a new passenger ship, even if she is going to be engaged on scheduled services, to undertake a cruise on delivery, partly to test all the systems and eliminate teething troubles, but also as a way of introducing her to the travel and trade press. Examples would be the *Queen Mary's* inaugural cruise on 14 May 1936 prior to her first Atlantic crossing on 27 May, and the *France*, which made an inaugural cruise to the West Indies on 29 January 1962 prior to the start of her transatlantic service.

Permanent departures of passenger ships have merited the same treatment, if for different reasons. Devotees can have a nostalgic farewell. The departure of *Queen Elizabeth 2* for Dubai in November 2008 is a notable example, for a series of farewell cruises of differing duration were offered to her devoted followers.

It is interesting to note that the *Royal Princess* was doused with a bottle of water from Southampton prior to her launch from a dry dock in Helsinki. The *Royal Princess* was later officially named by the Princess of Wales in Southampton in November 1984. This occasion was the first example in Southampton of a recent trend for the launching and naming of a new ship to be considered as separate events. Bringing the new ship from the builders to be officially named in a large passenger port means that a celebrity can perform the task before a sizeable audience and the ship owners can gain maximum publicity from the celebration. The most extreme example may be that of the *Crown Princess* which, after having undertaken several Mediterranean cruises, sailed from Southampton to New York to be officially named by the actress Sophia Loren in September 1990.

There was a step change in the size of cruise ships which is generally attributed to the arrival of the 70,000 ton *Norway* (formerly the *France*) on the scene in 1980 after conversion by her new owners. She visited Southampton in this new role in May before going to a new operating base in the United States, from which she sailed to the Caribbean where she was known as the first 'super ship'. There are undoubted advantages with larger ships: enhanced stability; more space and greater facilities for passengers, together with economies of scale. One disadvantage, of course, is that a very large vessel may be unable to enter some ports where a smaller ship could go. Big, however, remains beautiful: *Freedom of the Seas*, launched in 2006, is 154,407 tonnes; *Oriana* of 1995 is 69,153 tonnes; *Canberra* of 1961 was 49,073 tons; *Andes* of 1936 was 27,000 tons; and *Prinzessin Victoria Luise* of 1901 was only 4,409 tons. The most modern leviathans have no trouble entering Southampton of course, and the port retains its supremacy in the cruising league table with 289 cruise calls in 2008. Its nearest British rivals are Dover and Harwich. With 40 per cent of the UK market and some 900,000 cruise passengers passing through, Southampton entirely dominates the cruising scene.

In 1933, Andrews' garages organised a 'Gangway to garage' collection and delivery service where the firm would look after a car while its owner was away on a cruise. This facility proved popular and in September 1962, the *Shipping Guide* reported that 284 passengers'

Andrews' original dockside garage at 7 Berth. Outside is the 1921 Docks Garage Service Pump from which Pratt's motor spirit was dispensed by hand from the quayside to imported vehicles. At this time, Andrews Brothers were also storing cars for customers who were away on voyages, and packed and unpacked cars travelling with their owners. (Author)

cars were looked after while they were on-board the *Canberra* for a seven-day cruise. This was at the time the largest number of private vehicles associated with one specific cruise.

Late in 2002, the UK's first ever cruise exhibition, Cruise Expo, was held in the QE II Terminal. In July that year Southampton was nominated, for the first time, for two awards at the Miami Cruise Conference. These awards, for the quality of the facilities at the port, meant that Southampton became 'Northern Europe's Most Efficient Terminal Operator', and 'Northern Europe's Best Turnaround Port'. While these may be of little interest to the general public, they are a considerable accolade and mark Southampton as having truly established itself as a market leader in the world of cruising.

## TROOPING

The passing of military forces through Southampton has a long history. Roman troops must have landed in the area of Southampton to support their local base of Clausentum, and for onward passage to the city of Venta Belgarum, now Winchester. The army of Richard I departed for the Third Crusade from Southampton in the twelfth century and the troops of Edward III and Henry V left these shores to fight and win the Battles of Crecy in 1346 and Agincourt in 1415.

The value of Southampton as a port for the assembly and embarkation of soldiers continued unabated into modern times. From the earliest days of the 'modern' Docks, troops and troopships, or at least requisitioned merchant ships, were assembled and despatched to the Crimea in 1854 and virtually every other conflict in which Britain has been involved since. During the Crimean War, P&O alone transported 100,000 men and 20,000 horses, and other companies such as Royal Mail were heavily involved too.

The importance of Egypt to Britain had increased following the opening of the Suez Canal in 1869. This new route for shipping, moving from Europe to the Far East, halved the journey time between Britain and India, but a rise in local tension resulted in a British attack on Egypt in 1882. On Wednesday 9 August 1882, Queen Victoria arrived from East Cowes on-board the Royal Yacht *Alberta* to inspect the troop transports lying at 30-33 Berths before they sailed for Egypt. She was accompanied by the Princess Beatrice and the Duchess of Connaught, the Prince and Princess of Wales and their family, and the Duke of Cambridge. Her Majesty went aboard the largest of the eleven transports which collectively carried 3,439 officers and men and 2,002 horses.

Such was the facility for handling troops that, in 1895, the government made Southampton the port for handling all troop movements in peacetime. At that time over 50,000 troops and their equipment were conveyed each year, to and from far flung corners of the Empire. Soon after the government decision to focus this traffic on Southampton, a new system was adopted to speed the passage through the port. Put into operation for the first time during the Boer War, troop train movements were coordinated with the arrival or departure of the ships, so that troops could embark or disembark immediately from the quayside rather than encamp on the fringes of town and await their transport. Almost all of the vessels conveying troops and supplies for this conflict, amounting to 528,000 personnel and 27,922 horses, left from Southampton. The hired transports, of which 476 arrived and 419 departed, were in addition to the regular services to South Africa which were already in existence and which continued to sail with medical staff and other supplies for the war effort.

This large-scale exercise was a convenient rehearsal for the First World War and proved the capabilities of the port. When war broke out, Southampton was again to play its part, although under slightly different circumstances. The government took over the operation of the port and declared it to be the No.1 Port of Embarkation, effectively suspending all commercial activity. The Docks handled the movement of 7,689,510 personnel, 856,492 horses and mules and 3,381,274 tons of stores and ammunition in 16,291 ships. A transport shed had been made available for the Admiralty and War Office at 34 Berth and had been in use since 1903. The provision of facilities to the war effort during the First World War included the handing over of the recently created Tender Station at 50 Berth for use as a gun repair depot by the Army Ordnance Corps.

Very late in the war, the War Department also commandeered the facilities of the Harbour Board and a military jetty was constructed to the west of the Royal Pier in 1917. This was connected to what is now Central Station by a line running along Western Esplanade, from which rail vehicles were shunted directly onto train ferries and conveyed to Dieppe. After the war, surplus military equipment was returned by the same means and the jetty remained as a structure until the construction of the New Docks.

When conditions had returned to normal after the First World War, peacetime troop movements resumed but the overall numbers of troops involved declined a little to 49,000. The inaugural express service of Cunard from Southampton to New York began on 14 June 1919 when *Aquitania* sailed. She was not carrying ordinary passengers but

5,000 Canadian troops, effectively continuing the work she had done in her sailings from Southampton during the war. There was an eight-month season for these movements by conventional troop ship, running from September to April. From 1936 troop trains meeting vessels at the New Docks were able to use the new Millbrook loop line.

Conditions were different during the Second World War. Vital supplies were handled and important war work carried out, but only the Western Docks were taken over completely for military use and became the United States Army Transportation Corps' 14th Major Port. From D-Day to the end of the war, 3.5 million service personnel and 3.5 million tons of stores and equipment passed through the Docks.

Many passenger ships familiar before the war continued to use the port, but assumed different roles. *Winchester Castle* had been engaged in trooping and had been used as an assault training ship, later playing a considerable part in landings made by forces in Madagascar, North Africa and southern France. *Llangibby Castle* sailed regularly during 1944 with British and American troops for Normandy, and *Llandovery Castle* and the Royal Mail Line *Atlantis* were both hospital ships.

A return to normal peacetime operations took a very long time, especially because troops not only had to be moved round the world but very large numbers of refugees and displaced persons had to be dealt with, as well as prisoners of war to be repatriated. One of the last duties of both *Queen Elizabeth* and *Queen Mary* before their release from war service, on 6 March and 29 September 1946 respectively, was to carry GI war brides across the Atlantic in order to reunite them with their American husbands in the US.

On the peacetime trooping front, work pressed ahead with the building of new unified premises for the Ministry of Transport's Sea Transport Division. This was located on a four acre (1.6 hectare) site in West Bay Road in the Western Docks, and was designed to handle the whole of the local administration and servicing of troopships. The office block accommodated the Divisional Sea Transport Officer, the Senior Inspecting Officer and the Stores Officer, and their respective staffs.

The main building was for storage of bedding and linen, lifebelts, cargo handling equipment and ships' fittings. It also housed facilities for fumigating, sorting and repairing bedding. The site had its own railway siding and road vehicle loading bays, and came into operation in early 1954. In May 1958, the government again decided that all troopships engaged on long sea voyages were to be based in Southampton, as had been the case before the Second World War. In the intervening period, the *Oxfordshire* and *Devonshire* of Bibby Line had operated from Liverpool.

Many companies supplied vessels for this service. The principal ones were P&O, British India and Bibby Line, but the Ministry of Transport also owned some dedicated ships, such as *Empire Trooper* and *Empire Orwell*. These were operated on its behalf by British India and Orient Line respectively. Many, if not most, of the companies associated with Southampton have provided troop transport at some time. In 1951, the Charlton Steamship Co. contributed *Charlton Star* and in the mid-1950s, Cunard provided three ships, *Samaria*, *Scythia* and *Franconia* to carry Canadian troops. Additional work in moving large numbers of military personnel arose in 1953, as it had on similar occasions in the past when contingents of Commonwealth troops arrived to take part in the coronation procession of Queen Elizabeth II.

The writing was, however, on the wall for this sort of activity. Overseas posts were diminishing as the Empire shrank and the pioneering experiment that had proved the superiority of aircraft for the movement of troops had taken place in Southampton some eighteen months before the opening of the Sea Transport Division's new headquarters. In 1962 the government announced that all future peacetime troop movements would be made by air and, when the *Oxfordshire* returned to Southampton from Malta on 19 December that year, trooping by sea came to an end. The Sea Transport offices remained empty for nearly two years, but were converted into a training school by the Ministry of Labour, delivering classes to the building and engineering trades from September 1964.

An exhibition to commemorate the passing of the port's long association with military transport was put on in the Ocean Terminal in late 1963. The following companies, in addition to those already mentioned, were listed as having participated at some time: Anchor Line; Blue Funnel; British & Commonwealth; Chandris; Donaldson; Ellerman; Furness Withy; Lamport & Holt; New Zealand Shipping Co.; Pacific Steam Navigation Co.; Prince Line; Royal Mail; and Shaw, Savill & Albion.

The Empress Dock was the principal point of arrival and departure in later years. One company to lose by the cessation of trooping by sea was the ice cream manufacturer T. Wall & Sons Ltd In 1954, the company's house journal had reported that British soldiers about to embark on outward-bound troop ships had a great liking for their product.

Military equipment is still handled, mostly in chartered vessels, at Marchwood Military Port. This was designed and built by the Royal Engineers in 1944 to supply the Allied landings in Normandy. The Royal Corps of Transport was formed in July 1965 and took over the operation of Marchwood from the Royal Engineers. By this time the prototype Landing Ship (Logistic), or LSL, *Sir Lancelot* was undergoing trials and LSLs started using Marchwood in 1966. These vessels were initially operated for the Army by British India Steam Navigation Co., but from 1970 operation passed to the Royal Fleet Auxiliary. The Army first experimented with ISO containers in the summer of 1968, loading them on an LSL by means of a hired crane and slings, but the use of containers grew over the following decade and Military Container Services was formed in April 1978. Marchwood gained ro-ro facilities in the 1970s and was extensively rebuilt and modernised in 1988.

The Southampton Division offices and depot of Wall's Ice Cream in Millbrook Road, photographed in around 1948. T. Wall & Sons were major suppliers of ice cream to shipping lines and also had a café in Central Road. (Reproduced with kind permission of Unilever, from an original in the Unilever Archives)

# Principal Shipping Companies using the Port

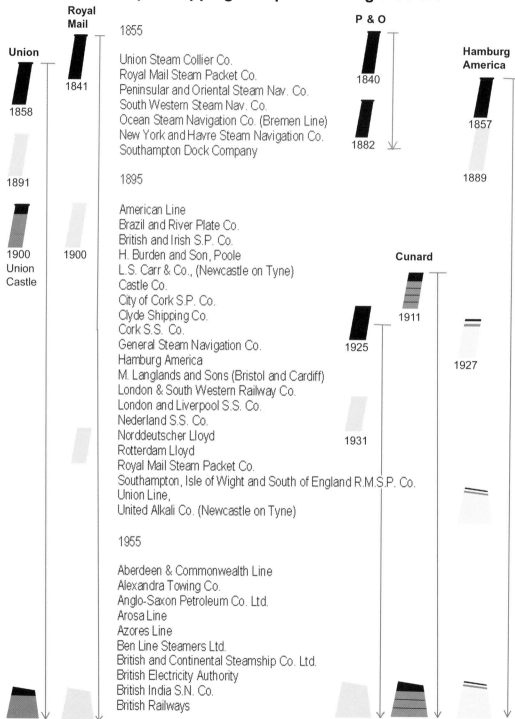

**Union**

1858

1891

1900
Union
Castle

**Royal Mail**

1841

1900

**P & O**

1840

1882

**Hamburg America**

1857

1889

1927

**Cunard**

1911

1925

1931

1855

Union Steam Collier Co.
Royal Mail Steam Packet Co.
Peninsular and Oriental Steam Nav. Co.
South Western Steam Nav. Co.
Ocean Steam Navigation Co. (Bremen Line)
New York and Havre Steam Navigation Co.
Southampton Dock Company

1895

American Line
Brazil and River Plate Co.
British and Irish S.P. Co.
H. Burden and Son, Poole
L.S. Carr & Co., (Newcastle on Tyne)
Castle Co.
City of Cork S.P. Co.
Clyde Shipping Co.
Cork S.S. Co.
General Steam Navigation Co.
Hamburg America
M. Langlands and Sons (Bristol and Cardiff)
London & South Western Railway Co.
London and Liverpool S.S. Co.
Nederland S.S. Co.
Norddeutscher Lloyd
Rotterdam Lloyd
Royal Mail Steam Packet Co.
Southampton, Isle of Wight and South of England R.M.S.P. Co.
Union Line,
United Alkali Co. (Newcastle on Tyne)

1955

Aberdeen & Commonwealth Line
Alexandra Towing Co.
Anglo-Saxon Petroleum Co. Ltd.
Arosa Line
Azores Line
Ben Line Steamers Ltd.
British and Continental Steamship Co. Ltd.
British Electricity Authority
British India S.N. Co.
British Railways

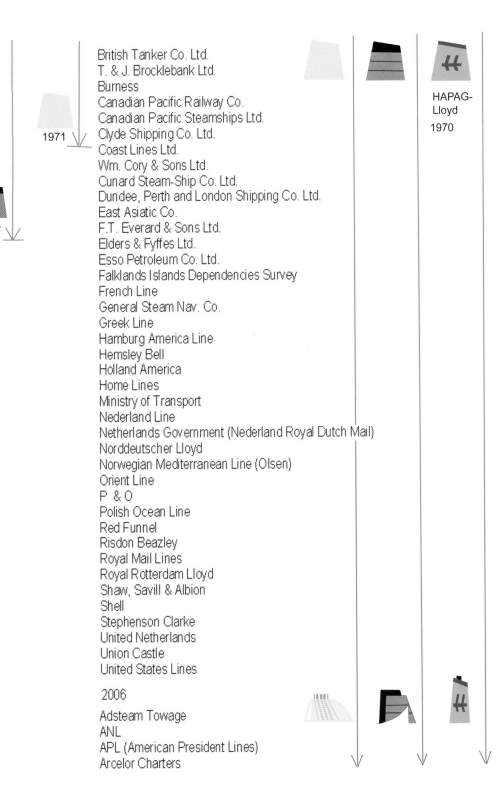

British Tanker Co. Ltd.
T. & J. Brocklebank Ltd.
Burness
Canadian Pacific Railway Co.
Canadian Pacific Steamships Ltd.
Clyde Shipping Co. Ltd.
Coast Lines Ltd.
Wm. Cory & Sons Ltd.
Cunard Steam-Ship Co. Ltd.
Dundee, Perth and London Shipping Co. Ltd.
East Asiatic Co.
F.T. Everard & Sons Ltd.
Elders & Fyffes Ltd.
Esso Petroleum Co. Ltd.
Falklands Islands Dependencies Survey
French Line
General Steam Nav. Co.
Greek Line
Hamburg America Line
Hemsley Bell
Holland America
Home Lines
Ministry of Transport
Nederland Line
Netherlands Government (Nederland Royal Dutch Mail)
Norddeutscher Lloyd
Norwegian Mediterranean Line (Olsen)
Orient Line
P & O
Polish Ocean Line
Red Funnel
Risdon Beazley
Royal Mail Lines
Royal Rotterdam Lloyd
Shaw, Savill & Albion
Shell
Stephenson Clarke
United Netherlands
Union Castle
United States Lines

2006

Adsteam Towage
ANL
APL (American President Lines)
Arcelor Charters

1971

1977

HAPAG-Lloyd
1970

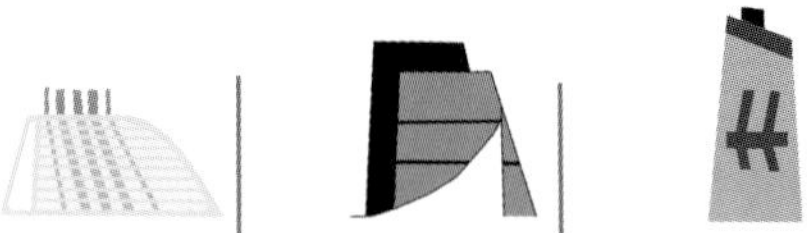

CCNI
China Shipping Group
Clydeport Shipping
CMA CGM (Compagnie Maritime d'Affretement / Compagnie Général Maritime)
Comanav
Cosco
CP Ships (Canadian Pacific)
Cunard Line
Eukor
Eurofeeders
Evergreen Marine
Flota Suardiaz
Fred Olsen Cruise Line
Grimaldi Line
Hapag-Lloyd
Hoegh
Hyundai Merchant Marine
K-Line
Lykes lines
Lys Line
Maersk
MISC
Mitsui OSK Lines
MOL
Norasia
NYK (Nippon Yusen Kaisha)
OOCL (Orient Overseas Container Line)
P & O Cruises
Red Funnel
Royal Caribbean
Royal Research Ships
Saga Holidays
TMM Lines
Thomson Cruises
United European Car Carriers
Wallenius Wilhelmsen Logistics UK
Whittaker Tankers

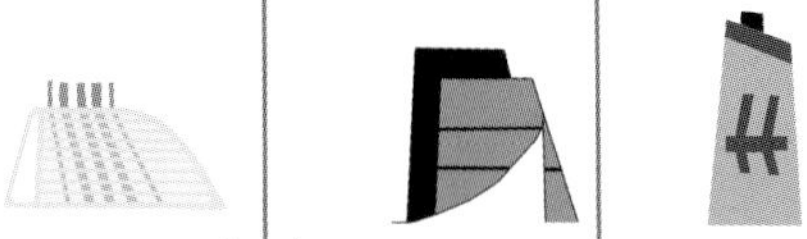

# 4

# MERCHANDISE

## FREE TRADE ZONE

Following the creation of opportunities arising from the 1984 Finance Act, Southampton Free Trade Zone, Britain's first Freeport, opened in August 1984. It attracted sixty customers in its first year of operation. The FTZ was initially sited on a 32 acre (12.5 hectare) site surrounded by a security fence and centred on 101 and 102 Berths. The idea was that the new development would become an entrepôt for the distribution of goods throughout Northern Europe and would attract custom because the system improved cash flow for users by deferring payment of import duties, VAT, etc., and simplified documentation. The high security also brought insurance benefits and led to intriguing signs at the entrances which proclaimed that 'you are now leaving the Customs Territory of the European Community'. Southampton Free Trade Zone Ltd, when created, was a partnership between Associated British Ports, which held 51 per cent, and Trafalgar House, Kleinwort Benson and Ocean Cory.

The initial plans incorporated a second phase of development in the form of a park for high technology industries operating within the FTZ and along the same lines. In fact, after the experimental period Southampton Free Trade Zone Ltd, which was wholly owned by ABP from 1996, was relocated to a 6.8 acre (2.75 hectare) site at Dock Gate 20, where there has been a concentration on the storage and distribution of high-value, mainly electronic, goods. Today it is one of five such zones in the United Kingdom and is part of ABP Connect.

## FRUIT AND VEGETABLES

Today we concern ourselves about the damage to the environment resulting from the use of aircraft to bring fresh produce from far-off lands. It is only in relatively recent times that this produce has become available to British purchasers when out of season in the UK, or because the climate in which they are grown is quite different from ours.

Although Oakley & Watling Ltd, the wholesale fruit and vegetable distributor, can trace its origins back to at least the seventeenth century, its sphere of operation during the early years was severely limited and involved the carriage of locally grown produce to local markets. Even during the Crimean War, local businessman Mr Page offered not to supply carrots and cabbages to military hospitals in Turkey and the Crimea, but to supply seed so that fresh vegetables could be grown on the spot. A large quantity of seed was carried from Southampton on the *Medway* for this purpose in 1854.

A post-war publication of the Fruit & Produce Exchange of Great Britain Ltd put the position very eloquently by stating that, 'The history of the introduction into this country of many of the fruits we enjoy today is bound up with the great adventures of the past'. There is a tendency for new foodstuffs to be introduced as exotic luxuries, affordable only to the well-off and only gradually to become abundant and commonplace. Oranges, for example, which had been imported as a luxury item for many years, were the only fruit imported from overseas by the Ministry of Food during the Second World War as they were robust enough to withstand the rigours of the journey, kept reasonably well and could be used to provide orange juice. Infants and children received a special ration of juice, considered to be necessary to their health when so many other foods were rationed or in short supply.

Regular shipments of citrus fruit to Southampton from the recently formed Union of South Africa did not begin until 1910, although the first orange trees had been planted there some 250 years before. The 300th anniversary of the foundation of the fruit growing industry was marked on 13 June 1954 when the Mayor of Pretoria presented a commemorative scroll to the Mayor of Southampton in recognition of the importance of the town to the South African export trade

The first experimental shipment of deciduous fruit from South Africa to Southampton arrived on *Grantully Castle* in 1889. While it is not recorded what went wrong with that first cargo, it was later recorded that the first successful shipment was brought on *Drummond Castle* in 1892, using special 'fruit chambers' which had been constructed in the hold. The regular supply of apples, pears, plums and peaches, which have a season from December to June, did not start until the spring of 1907. In that year, a total of 10,000 cases of fruit arrived at Southampton, a figure that continued to rise every year except for those when Britain was at war. In 1967 for example, which was not a peak year, over 8.5 million cases of deciduous fruit and nearly 4.5 million cases of citrus fruit were brought here, which represented 92.8 per cent and 53 per cent respectively of the quantities sent to Britain.

The first commercial appearance of the banana was in 1884 and people in London and Liverpool were the first to experience them. Bananas made their first appearance in Southampton in 1903 when the *Oracabessa* of Elders & Fyffes discharged 33,078 stems at Shed 25. In fact, regular traffic did not commence until 5 May 1931 with a crop from the Canaries, followed in July by Colombian fruit. Quantities of fruit imported increased annually until the traffic in bananas via the Port of Southampton stopped in 1939. Bananas were unavailable in Britain during the Second World War. In 1953 the Ministry of Food deregulated the supply and Elders & Fyffes resumed contact with the *Viator* on 1 February. An astonishing 2.5 million stems were imported that year, a quantity that immediately surpassed the previous record that had been set in 1935.

The first purpose-built terminal for banana traffic was Shed 35 at 25 Berth, construction of which began in 1933. This had pocketed belt elevators which were positioned in the ships' holds to lift the stems, thus reducing manual effort and protecting the bananas. The terminal was modernised in 1957 when the elevators and conveyors were made shore-based and new offices and a reception hall for passengers was added. A new unloading machine feeding six railway tracks (four for green bananas and two for ripe ones) was first put into operation on 10 January 1960 when *Changuinola* discharged 67,000 stems from the Cameroons.

Further modernisation was carried out in 1969 when roller conveyors were used to guide the packages of bananas toward the elevators, which in turn had their capacity doubled in order to handle the same volume more slowly and thus reduce damage. This last series of adaptations was necessary because of a change in the method of shipment. When the *Calamares* arrived from the West Indies in July 1966, she discharged 75,736 stems of bananas and 85,130 cartons. By September the following year, all bananas were being packed in cartons which reduced damage and made the fruit easier to handle.

Bananas came from other countries too. Royal Mail brought Brazilian bananas from 1935 until their shipping services ended and from the late 1940s Israeli bananas were imported. In 1948 Fred Olsen and Co. re-established pre-war links with Southampton with a new fruit service from Morocco. From 1925, Australian soft fruit arrived in the holds of Aberdeen & Commonwealth ships, coinciding with the import of apples from the North Pacific and Nova Scotia. Spanish grapes and oranges first appeared here in 1920.

The Canary Fruit
Terminal with the
Rank Hovis flour mill
in the background. The
floating crane *Canute*
can also be seen in the
distance. (Associated
British Ports)

In November 1949, two Scandinavian companies, Fruit Express Line from Norway
and Uddevalla Rederi A/B from Sweden, started the trade in tomatoes from the Canaries,
followed towards the end of 1957 by Navecome Navagaco e Commercia (London) Ltd

The first commercial production of tomatoes in the Channel Islands had been in 1874,
when they were brought to Southampton on railway steamers, the railway-operated
steam ferries that provided regular communication with the islands. New potatoes, also a
product of Jersey, likewise arrived on railway boats.

The import of Scottish potatoes had been a speciality of Thomas Cowan since 1896.
From 1919 this company became part of the Dundee, Perth & London Shipping Co., the
only coastal shipping company to use the main docks rather than Town Quay.

The growth both in volume of traffic and in the size of ships led to the handling of
South African produce at a new terminal and deep-water anchorage at 102 Berth in the
Western Docks. This was to receive ships of the Union Castle line that had the contract
to handle the whole of the South African fruit crop. As the original transit shed had been
destroyed during the Second World War, a replacement two-storey building was designed
by J.H. Jellett, the Docks Engineer, and opened in 1956. This building was modernised in
1972 so that road vehicles could load on the landward side, which made it much easier
and quicker to unload and convey produce to its destination.

Almost twenty years later, and again in order to increase access for large ships and
cargoes, the Canary Fruit Terminal located at 104 Berth was created as a common user
terminal and was opened in December 1991 by the Mayor of Southampton, Councillor
Brian Welch. It was the first fruit terminal to be constructed in the South since changes
in EC import regulations, and was the most modern at the time with a temperature-
controlled capacity of 10,695sq. m (115,000sq. ft). The building was refurbished and
extended in 1995. An agreement had been concluded with the Federation of Canary
Island Producers in 1994 to handle all the islands' produce brought to the UK, and this
was renewed in 2000 and again in 2005. Over 100,000 pallets of fresh produce are handled here in season by Southampton Fruit Handling (Operations) Ltd

The Windward Terminal was erected at 101 Berth in 1993 as the result of an agreement
with Geest PLC to bring all the bananas imported from the Windward Islands and Costa

Rica through Southampton, thus bringing half the country's supply of the fruit through the port. The building was opened by the Secretary of State for Transport, the Rt Hon. John McGregor. It was constructed by Taylor Woodrow on a 9 acre (3.6 hectare) site giving 5,580sq. m (60,000sq. ft) of temperature controlled space and 1,860sq. m (20,000sq. ft) of covered cargo space. The first of a new generation of deep-draught cargo ships, the *Geest St Lucia*, inaugurated services. Unfortunately, Geest suffered severe difficulties with loss of crops through hurricane and disease and closed the banana division in 1996.

By the 1920s Southampton had gained a reputation as a centre for the importation of fresh fruit. Apart from other advantages, easy road and rail connections reduced the time taken in the distribution of perishable produce to London and provincial centres. Fruit was sold either by private treaty or by auction through the auction rooms at 14 Berth in the Inner Dock. Although these premises were lost during the Second World War, the first post-war fruit auction in the country was held in Southampton on 9 May 1950. The *Fruit Trades Journal* reported in 1969 that Southampton was then the fourth largest port in the country, both in terms of tonnage and value of fruit handled. By 1993, Southampton had become the largest fruit handling port in the UK and still remains a major player in the business.

## MEAT

Almost from the beginning of its history, Southampton Docks handled live cattle for which holding pens or lairages were provided to contain the animals on the dockside. Much of this traffic arose from the Channel Islands and by the late nineteenth century the cattle were transported in railway steamers equipped for the purpose.

Although by this period refrigerated ships had enabled New Zealand lamb or Argentine beef to be brought to this country in a frozen state, there was nowhere at Southampton to keep the meat safely without defrosting before it could be distributed. The potential value of Southampton as a meat distribution centre became apparent with the arrival of American Line in 1893 and the recently formed International Cold Storage & Lairage Co. Ltd began construction of a refrigerated store at 40 Berth in March 1900. Built along futuristic lines, from Hennebique Ferro-concrete, it was 400ft (122m) long and 100ft (30.5m) wide, with a railway siding giving accommodation for twenty-two refrigerated vans. It had a net capacity of 1.2 million cu. ft (101,933 cu. m). Adjacent steam-powered ammonia compressors provided refrigeration and the company also generated its own electricity for lighting on site. At the start the company provided lairage accommodation for 1,500 head of cattle and had its own abattoir, but this was abandoned in 1908 because of declining traffic. The head of the first bull to be slaughtered on site was mounted as a trophy and kept for many years. The name of the company was changed in 1910 to the International Cold Storage & Ice Co. Ltd A quarter of a century after it was built, Southampton's cold store was still the largest in Europe, and there were only four larger examples worldwide.

The cold store housed large consignments of foodstuffs during both World Wars. Supplies of many foods were rationed during the Second World War as it became increasingly difficult to bring supplies from overseas. This made the Docks a major target, and in November 1940 the cold store was lost during a bombing raid. Images of the burning building show the size of the loss, including a large quantity of the nation's butter supply, which only added fuel to the flames.

The International Cold Store at 40 Berth early in the twentieth century, showing the adjoining power plant with its chimney. (Author)

As early as 1947, not long after hostilities ended, the International Cold Storage & Ice Co. had drawn up plans for a replacement facility to be built at 108 Berth. The Dock Handbook of that year proudly announced that 'work has commenced' on a modern replacement that was intended to be operational by 1949. In fact, the building, erected by the British Transport Commission and operated by the company, did not come into use until 16 July 1958 when the *Brisbane Star* of Blue Star Line unloaded 1,100 tons of meat, 200 tons of butter and 15,000 cases of apples. The ground floor of the new building was a transit shed, and at this time only the first and second floors were insulated. The top floor was not completed until April 1967. The structure was intended to 're-establish Southampton as a leading distribution centre for refrigerated cargoes', and must have been successful because in 1969 the New Zealand Meat Producers' Board decided to quadruple the quantity of meat exported to Britain through the Port of Southampton.

In May 1959, the name of the company was changed to International Cold Storage Co. Ltd Dropping the '& Ice' led to the appearance of the newspaper headline 'Defrosted', although, of course, the company continued to offer a refrigerated storage facility for imported meat.

Trade with nations that had exported through Southampton before the war was revived with the return of Argentine beef on the *Alcantara* in January 1954. Four years later, on 17 October 1958, a consignment of beef from what was then known as Bechuanaland, now Botswana, arrived on the *Pretoria Castle*.

The effects of the Second World War, both in terms of recovery from the financial cost as well as the effects of severe and sustained bombing, lasted for many years. In February 1959 the last remnants of the old Cold Store that had blazed so spectacularly in 1940 were removed, while the cargo shed at 41 Berth was extended to cover the site of the earlier engine house only in 1962.

The new cold store had been designed with an area suitable for 'quick frozen' foods. Nine years prior to its opening, the firm of Oakley & Watling, which had specialised in provisioning ships with fresh fruit and vegetables, had begun to supply frozen produce.

By 1951, Southern Frozen Products Ltd were advertising their products, which now included meat, fish, poultry and game, to shipping lines. The dock Cold Store finally became redundant once refrigerated stores, road vehicles and containers became commonplace.

## GRAIN

The grain trade through Southampton started in 1845 in anticipation of the repeal of import duty in 1846. The initial purpose of Inner Dock, which opened in 1851, was to handle grain and coal and two of its earliest buildings were granaries. After the takeover of the Docks by the London & South Western Railway in 1892, storage capacity was increased by the construction of three new granaries and the addition of bucket elevators to raise the grain from ships' holds. Even at this time, cargoes could be handled either in bulk or in bags.

The next major development was the construction of the technically advanced, electrically powered flour mill built for Joseph Rank Ltd in the centre of the reclaimed land of the Docks Extension. Construction of the Solent Flour Mills began in 1932, even before the dock extension was completed. The mill became operational in August 1934, although it was not officially opened by the Mayor until 4 October. This imposing series of buildings was the first, and for a time only, group of buildings on the new estate and, like the equally monumental Cold Store, was badly damaged during the Second World War. Originally there was a flour mill, a provender mill, a silo and warehouse, of which the warehouse and flour mill were completely destroyed by enemy action. The site also had its own 260ft (79m) deep artesian well supplying the mill with water. After the war, the need to feed the country made reconstruction of the mill a priority and the new complex, which was completed in July 1950 and operational in 1951, incorporated a flour mill of double the original size and a warehouse three times as big. At this time, Solent Flour Mill was the largest in the South outside London, but a seven-storey extension was added in 1955 and new 106 ft (32m) high silos were added in 1964, which added 15,000 tons to the storage capacity. Rank's became part of RHM Flour Mills Ltd on 6 September 1971 but continued to invest in the Southampton mill. By 1986 almost a quarter of the grain processed by the firm was coming from Canada, but Britain was fast becoming a net grain-exporting country and Southampton had already become its biggest grain-exporting port. In the twenty-first century, following further modernisation, Solent Mills has become the largest of the eleven remaining Rank Hovis mills and one of the most advanced in Europe.

Southampton Grain Silos Ltd was opened at 36 Berth in September 1983 by Princess Anne. Although built with eight silos, another nine, connected to the first, were brought into operation in 1987, giving a total capacity of 30,000 tons. This facility has been operated by a subsidiary of a French firm, Soufflet Agriculture Ltd, since 1995. Ships of up to 55,000 tons can berth alongside, there are computerised weighbridges and grain is automatically sampled and analysed on arrival.

Continental Grain (UK) Ltd was in operation at 47 Berth from August 1982 and had a capacity of 16,000 tons. This became the facility of Grainfarmers in the twenty-first century, although the site has since been redeveloped.

Very large shipments, mainly of wheat and of the order of 40,000 tons, have been made in individual vessels, mainly to the Far East and Middle East. One of the largest shipments to date was of 60,000 tonnes to China on the *Li Chan Hai* towards the end of 1995.

The flour mill of Rank Hovis, in its modern form after post-war reconstruction and the addition of extra silos. (Author)

With the advent of containers, a different way of thinking about cargoes has evolved. Commodities that won't go in a box are generally 'bulk' cargoes. There are commodities other than grain but related to food that are classed as 'agribulks', and it is no surprise that Southampton has developed the capacity to deal with these cargoes. Thus the Mulberry Terminal for animal feed and fertiliser storage intended for use by Usborne PLC and Continental Grain (UK) Ltd was opened by Sir Keith Stuart, Chairman of ABP, on 25 May 1995. The terminal was built by Brazier & Sons at 107 Berth, which is rail connected. In the late twentieth century it diversified still further so that it is now capable of handling aggregates.

## TIMBER

It was said in the mid-1920s that Southampton's continued prosperity was due to both the revival of the timber trade after the First World War and the return of P&O.

This dependence on timber continued after the creation of the New Docks, the second tenant of which was Montague L. Mayer Ltd, who from October 1936 were importing timber from the White Sea, the Baltic and British Columbia. Mayer's 2.5 acre (1 hectare) site was just north of the carriage cleaning shed and comprised a 434ft (132m) long storage shed of wooden construction, and a concrete and steel-framed saw mill, which was 122ft (37m) long. The company merged with International Timber to form Mayer International in 1982, was restructured and reverted to the old name in 1998, and since April 2002 has concentrated on manufactured panel products imported mainly from South America and the Far East and routed through Berth 107.

In the nineteenth century, there were two long timber sheds along the western side of what became Central Road, but these had been demolished by 1910. After the construction of Ocean Dock, 45 Berth was used for timber traffic, with timber that had been discharged into barges often being stored in the old Coal Dock. This work was undertaken by firms such as R. & J.H. Rea which had begun lighterage, the loading or discharging of a ship's cargo via barges, in 1895.

New timber sheds were erected at the back of 40 Berth in 1930 and one of the first ships to use this berth to discharge timber directly onto the quayside was the *Margareta* from British Columbia in February 1957.

An account of 1953 gives details of the types of timber imported at that time and some of their uses. Imports were about 70 per cent softwood. The account reads: softwood deals, batons and boards from Norway, Sweden and Russia with smaller amounts from Yugoslavia and Corsica; Douglas fir, hemlock, balsam pine, red cedar and spruce from British Columbia; Corsican beech, Siberian larchwood, ramin from Sarawak; maritime pine, ash, elm and beech from France; telegraph poles from Sweden and Finland; parana pine from Brazil; and sleeper and crossing timbers from British Columbia. There were occasional specialist imports of woods like jarrah and karri, such as the shipment brought by the *Boogabilla* from Western Australia in June 1960.

The importance of Town Quay in respect of imported timber should not be over-looked. The largest single shipment ever received at the quay was 3,000 tons of Russian timber which arrived on the freighter *Murmashi* in the summer of 1969. And one log from a consignment of greenheart discharged by the *Harbo* in 1972 was recorded as being 71ft (21.6m) long and 21 inches (533mm) square.

Bulk cargo being unloaded by grab at 207 Berth in the Western Docks (Associated British Ports)

Empress Road is in the foreground with the camera pointing towards 34, 35 and 36 Berths on the far side of the timber sheds. Prince of Wales Dry Dock is difficult to see because of the low camera angle. The photograph was taken after the railway grouping of 1923, which was also the year in which J. Samuel White & Co. set up its ship repair business in Southampton. The name can be seen on the roof of the sheds in the middle distance on the right of the photograph. (Stan Roberts)

Channel Islands flying boat over Town Quay in about 1926. There are ships here of the British & Irish Steam Packet Co., Coast Lines Ltd and Clyde Shipping Co. Ltd (Bitterne Local History Society)

# CARS

Southampton has handled motor vehicles for very many years, traffic in which generally falls into two groups: either short sea voyages where the vehicle itself is not imported or exported but makes a return journey, generally on-board a ferry, or the import and export of vehicles – mainly new, but not always – as an item of trade, a commodity.

Southampton has been associated with three separate phases of the ferry trade and the carriage of vehicles carrying either goods or holiday makers. The first vehicle transporters were the railway ferries which were designed or adapted for car carrying only in their later years. The second phase took place in the 1960s and 1970s when private companies employed new ferry designs on an extended network of European routes to cater for the newly adventurous families keen to explore the Continent under their own steam. Finally in the 1990s came the revival of Continental car ferry operations by Sealink Stena Line using the *Stena Normandy* to cross the Channel between Southampton and Cherbourg.

Apart from the Hythe Ferry, the only remaining ferry operating out of Southampton is the purely local, but nevertheless heavily used, service operated by Red Funnel to the Isle of Wight.

## *Ferry and Freight Transport*

Southampton has the unique distinction of having been the first port in Britain to handle a vehicle with an internal combustion engine. This was the Panhard et Levassor car ordered by the Hon. Evelyn Henry Ellis in 1894. It was completed in June 1895 and shipped from Paris to Southampton. The car subsequently went by rail to Micheldever Station, where it was unloaded and driven by Ellis and a colleague on 6 July to Ellis's home 'Rosenau' in Datchet, which is now in Berkshire but was then in Buckinghamshire.

The port soon built on this experience. Some steam vehicles were sent to South Africa during the Boer War. The First World War, being the first fully mechanised war, saw motor vehicles handled as a matter of course and in very great numbers; a total of 177,953 were recorded as they passed through the port. That conflict introduced many service people to motoring and led directly to the development of the motoring excursion, or taking the car on holiday.

Passenger ferries have a long association with Southampton going back to the pre-railway era, linking the port with the Channel Islands and with France. After the First World War, those who had private cars increasingly wanted to take them abroad on holiday. 'At one time one or two cars a night were taken abroad, now even people with small cars want to go', noted the *Shipping Guide* of October 1926. In fact, in 1925, 2,696 cars were conveyed to and from the Continent from the Docks. The Southern Railway, which also owned Dover Docks, had noted the rise in demand for car ferry services and brought the first railway cross-Channel car ferry, *Autocarrier*, into operation there on 30 March 1930. This vessel had a capacity of only twenty-six cars, which still had to be craned on and off, but was an indication that the band of motorists was growing and that they were becoming more adventurous as the reliability of motor vehicles and the availability of fuel improved. In May 1949, following the end of the Second World War, *Autocarrier* reopened the seasonal Southampton-St Malo service and provided additional car-carrying space.

Four horse-power Panhard et Levassor motor car. This was the first internal combustion-engined vehicle imported into Britain, which arrived in Southampton in 1895. At the time people were unsure of the best arrangement for the components of a car, but the 'système Panhard', with an engine at the front driving the rear axle and with transverse rows of seats pointing forward, became the norm. The car can be seen in the Science Museum in London. (Author)

A 'Lifu' steam omnibus waiting by the ramp to the pontoon at the end of the Royal Pier. These oil-burning steam vehicles were made by the Liquid Fuel Engineering Co. Ltd of East Cowes between 1897 and 1900. (Brain collection)

Some of the needs of motorists were already being catered for as the Automobile Association opened its first office at 9 Berth in 1922 under the direction of their Port Officer, Miss Scott. The office moved from a wooden hut to larger premises in 1937 and, after an absence during the Second World War, returned to new offices in the same area in 1956. Andrews Brothers, as the firm of Andrews Shipside Services was then known, had noticed an opportunity as early as 1920 and advertised themselves from 7 Berth as 'the car packing specialists'. In the 1930s Andrews announced their innovative 'gangway to garage' service for the collection and delivery of the cars of customers who were perhaps going on a cruise or crossing the Channel on holiday. Vehicles were stored until their owners' return. These services were in addition to Andrews' more conventional role of motor-vehicle repairers and filling station. In fact, from about 1924, Andrews operated a mobile filling station to meet the imported cars of individual customers, fuel them and prepare them for the road. The vehicles used for this service changed several times in order to meet the increasing demand so that Bedford tankers, which were introduced in 1953, were exchanged for two 600 gallon (2,700 litre) Scammell 'Mechanical Horses' in 1964, and finally the 1,800 gallon (8,200 litre) mobile petrol tanker of 1974.

The railway steamers, which were nationalised in 1948, had not been keeping up with passenger needs, particularly the carriage of passengers' cars. For comfort and speed, the LSWR had introduced the first passenger ships to be driven by geared turbines, the *Hantonia* and *Normannia*, and these valiant ships had continued to sail to France until its capitulation to the invading Nazis in 1940.

From early 1961, the fashion for motor scooters was fed by imports from Italy which were taken to Le Havre and then by railway steamer to Southampton. This traffic, however innovative, was insufficient to save the service and in January 1962 the passenger service to and from the Channel Islands was transferred to Weymouth. This was only the first service to be lost, as the railway service to Le Havre ended with the arrival of *St Patrick* on 10 May 1964, and finally the St Malo service ended in September the same year.

The first modern drive-on, drive-off car, passenger and freight ferry to use Southampton as a base was Thoresen's *Viking I*, which departed for Cherbourg from Outer Dock on 11 May 1964. The line had been in negotiations with British Transport Docks Board since December 1962 for facilities for a car ferry service to France and, as Outer Dock was rapidly becoming redundant for other purposes, modern facilities could be provided at 6 Berth. An advertisement of Thoresen's prior to the introduction of the service shows the motivation and some of the perceived advantages:

> The modern, fast ferries, with their 11 line 'drive straight through' facilities at bow and stern, cut embarking and disembarking times to a matter of seconds a car… Once on board, the holiday really begins. These new, fully stabilized ships offer luxury liner-type holiday travel, including Continental restaurant, cafeteria, bars and duty free shops.

They were therefore a great advance on the railway ferries, particularly in terms of passenger comfort, and made European holidays by car an attractive proposition for ordinary families.

In 1965, British Transport Docks Board sought the approval of the Minister of Transport to provide two more terminals for ro-ro ferries, as they became known. These were duly constructed for the Swedish Lloyd Bilbao service, which began on 5 April 1967 with the maiden voyage of the *Patricia*, and the Normandy Ferries service to Le Havre, which began with the departure of the *Dragon* on 29 June that year. Somerfin Passenger Lines commenced a service to Algeciras with their vessel *Nili* in May 1965, and Seagull Ferries had introduced a ro-ro service to Le Havre in July 1965, both from a link-span bridge at 49 Berth, although this latter service was for freight only. From April 1966 the car ferry terminal near No. 6 Dry Dock also accommodated the service to Vigo and Gibraltar operated by Klosters Rederi. Modifications to Outer Dock were completed and it was renamed Princess Alexandra Dock in a ceremony that took place on 3 July 1967. Jersey Lines Ltd used the Princess Alexandra Dock for one season, commencing with the departure of *La Duchesse de Bretagne* on 7 April 1968, temporarily re-establishing a Channel Islands service, while from 18 May 1971 Southern Ferries, the parent company of Normandy Ferries, started a service to Lisbon, San Sebastian and Tangier. Then on 8 May 1974, Aznar Line began operating to Santander.

Thoresen Car Ferries celebrated the carriage of its millionth passenger on 4 November 1966, although the location of Southampton and the necessity of travelling at low speeds down the Solent and around the Isle of Wight to the open Channel was already being perceived as a difficulty. Holiday passengers taking their cars to

Cherbourg were heading mainly for the Normandy and Brittany coasts that were within easy reach of the port. In 1968 Thoresen merged with Townsend Ferries to create Townsend Thoresen.

The position regarding freight transport was somewhat different. Southampton's location, away from London and with easy access to the Midlands and, on the other side of the Channel, to western France and Spain, meant that there were many advantages to freight carriers using the route. By March 1967 Southampton was ahead of Dover in the number of lorries and trailers carried to Le Havre on what had become known as the 'Channel motorway'.

In September 1977, Swedish Lloyd withdrew its passenger ferry service to Bilbao. The container part of its operation, which had been operated by MacAndrews Shipping Co., was taken up by the ro-ro service of the United Baltic Co. operating their vessel *Goya*. The ship, which left Southampton from 3 Berth, also called in at Bordeaux, but the service was entirely for freight. Rolo Line had, from 1972, been operating a freight-only ro-ro service to Bilbao and Le Havre from the link-span bridge at 201 Berth and was joined in March 1980 by Interoll SA of Madrid with *Rollman,* a ro-ro freight service to Spain, Portugal and Italy. Freight was clearly the way forward for Southampton.

An alternative ferry service for passengers wishing to reach Spain was provided by Brittany Ferries who started a service from Plymouth to Santander in 1978. Passengers spent one night less on the ship than they did sailing from Southampton, and considering they had to do it on both the outward and return journeys, this added two days onto their holiday that would otherwise have been spent on-board the ship.

A car passenger and freight ferry service to Cherbourg was revived by Sealink Stena Line in June 1991, with *Stena Normandy* operating from 31 Berth. This ship, a larger and more opulent vessel than any that had previously been used, was popular with local people, but the venture was not commercially successful and stopped in 1996.

## Vehicle Imports and Exports

The *Shipping Guide* of March 1928 intimated that 'motor cars from the United States [were] brought unpacked in special ships'. In February 1937, the same publication recorded the importation of American cars to be a comparatively new traffic. The vehicles were brought into Southampton in the holds of Red Star ships and were received in quantities of 300 or so at a time. These imports arrived before the opening of the General Motors plant in the New Docks which, in late 1938, was intended to be that company's centre for the assembly, finishing and distribution of Chevrolet trucks and Opel cars.

The Second World War intervened, but the import of US-built vehicles continued. During the war, American military equipment was brought across the Atlantic to what the US Army Transportation Corps called its 14th Major Port. These vehicles were then sent across the Channel, particularly in the period after D-Day. On the night of 5 June 1944, 20,000 vehicles were included with the personnel and materials shipped from Southampton to France, and within a month the total number shipped across the Channel had reached 200,000 vehicles.

There were two principal methods employed at this time in the loading and unloading of vehicles from ships. Firstly, the vehicle could be dismantled and packed in a crate for ease of stowage and to avoid damage. This system, known as 'completely knocked down' (CKD), was the method favoured for shipment to South Africa until the end of the mail service. The other method was to position the wheels over nets and, by using a load spreader so as not to crush the sides of the vehicle, to hoist it on or off a ship. This was the method taught at the National Dock Labour Board training school in Southampton, when the outdoor 'landship' was created in late 1966 for this purpose. Dummy cargo, including an old car, was used to practice slinging techniques.

During the Second World War, the landing ship and landing craft had been perfected in order to land troops, vehicles and equipment in shallow water so that rapid progress up the beachhead could be achieved. The idea that vehicles could be driven on and off the ship under their own power was not entirely new, as train ferries taking railed vehicles by this means had been in operation for many years, mainly in sheltered waters. One need look no further than the Itchen ferry to see horse-drawn vehicles carried between Southampton and Woolston on a floating roadway. The first shipping line to exploit this concept for vehicle shipment in the post-war era was the Atlantic Steam Navigation Co. However, the company's only visits to Southampton between January and August 1947 with the ex-military *Empire Baltic* were to convey not motor vehicles but new railway wagons, which were destined for the SNCF, the French national railway, in Le Havre and US Army Transportation Corps locomotives to Yugoslavia.

In 1950, Southampton was selected as the port for the export of cars to Australia and soon South Africa and South America were added to the list, with New Zealand being a further addition in 1954. There was an export drive to rebuild the economy and cased vehicles sent to South Africa proclaimed 'Britain has made it' on the sides.

The abolition of post-war import restrictions in 1960 led to a rapid increase in the number of motor vehicles imported from overseas. On 20 January 1960 the first shipment of 1,025 Renaults was discharged at 106 Berth by the conventional slinging method, as Renault had acquired six former Liberty ships and converted them into car carriers. The company had chosen Southampton as its sole British import centre and established a servicing and distribution depot off West Bay Road in Western Docks. A few thousand Renault Dauphines had been imported before, but the lifting of import quotas in 1960 led to a rapid increase in the number of vehicles passing through the port. By 1990, when Renault celebrated the thirtieth anniversary of its connection with Southampton, more than 1 million of its products had been handled.

The steam-powered Itchen ferry commenced operations in 1837 and crossed the Itchen between Woolston and the neoclassical building on the Southampton shore. Small sailing vessels are moored in the foreground. (Private collection)

The Swedish firm of Wallenius converted their ship *Traviata* into a roll-on, roll-off car carrier in 1962 and used her to convey cars from Rouen to Southampton, with the first shipment arriving on 10 January 1963. She used side loading ramps, the first time that the roll-off method had been used here, and again the cargo was Renaults. By this means a flow of 200 cars per hour could be achieved and a second ship, *Rigoletto*, was added in March.

In 1978 unwanted old buildings in part of the Eastern Docks were demolished and Prince of Wales Dry Dock filled in to form a hard standing, incorporating drainage and tall floodlights, in order to store more cars. This work was done by Southern Counties Construction Co. and Amy Roadstone Corporation Ltd Use of the railway system for the bulk handling of cars for export began through the Western Docks in April 1979 with trainloads of 200 British Leyland vehicles. Car trains running to the Eastern Docks, again with British Leyland products from Cowley and Longbridge, started in May 1996.

In 1985 Nicholas Ridley, Secretary of State for Transport, opened a specialist facility for World Shipping & Freight Ltd to be used for pre-delivery inspection, rectification and enhancement of imported vehicles at 201-202 Berths. The first imports to be handled were Fiat and Lancia cars in December. From January 1993, this facility was operated by Southampton Vehicle Terminals Ltd Today ABP Connect operates a similar facility at Redbridge Vehicle Terminal.

Wallenius and Wilhelmsen amalgamated in 1999 to form the world's largest ro-ro carrier, Wallenius Wilhelmsen Lines. This new company handles cars in such volume that sufficient buffer storage on ground level was not available, and therefore an agreement was reached with ABP in February 2001 for the construction of a multi-deck terminal. Southampton International Vehicle Terminal, the first of its kind in the UK, was opened on 29 April 2002. It has five levels of 1 hectare each, with a capacity for 3,120 cars, and incorporates the most modern features such as bar-coding via computer for inventory control. The plaque unveiled on opening reads, 'This terminal is an example of how two different European companies can create a winning combination to the benefit of international trade'. A second multi-deck terminal of similar size followed in late 2005, which has since been joined by a third, all in the Eastern Docks.

Wallenius Wilhelmsen car carrier *Tijuca* photographed at 35 Berth in 2009, having discharged new high-speed passenger railway rolling stock from Japan. In the background are the seventeen grain silos of Southampton Grain Terminal at 36 Berth. (Associated British Ports)

The first multi-deck car storage terminal completed in 2002. There are now three. The most recent was completed in 2009 and is on European Way in the Eastern Docks, near the National Oceanography Centre. (Associated British Ports)

The ever-increasing number of vehicles has been handled by ever-larger ships. In 1965 Wallenius' *Carmen* was not only the largest car carrier, but the largest cargo ship using the Docks with a capacity to take 500 cars to the United States. By 1969, *Georgian Glory* had set the record by loading 1,650 cars for shipment to the United States and Canada. Now, in the early twenty-first century, vessels with a capacity to carry 6,000 cars are not uncommon. The total number of vehicles imported and exported annually from the port rose from 65,000 in 1975 to 250,000 in 1990 and 500,000 in 2002. And in 1998, Southampton became the country's premier vehicle handling port with 20 per cent of the market. There are now 740,000 vehicles handled per year and 198 acres (80 hectares) of dockland are allocated for temporary storage. Looking back, the turning point in Southampton's history, when it became a significant car import and export centre, occurred in 1975 when cars were first handled 'in considerable numbers'.

The management of large vehicles and wheeled plant became a major feature from 1996, although the first Euclid dumper exported to France left Southampton in April 1966. This was the R45 model, the largest produced in Britain at the time.

## CONTAINERS

### Beginnings

The idea of putting goods in a large box in order to protect them or to make handling easier is a very old one; for example, open-topped wooden containers had been used to transport coal on the Bridgewater Canal at the end of the eighteenth century.

To some extent concentrating goods like this has always been necessary. Grapes came in casks, tomatoes in trays or baskets, and these themselves might have been moved in relative bulk from quayside to warehouse on wooden tables, a sort of early pallet. These were picked up and transported on the fleet of Elwell-Parker battery electric vehicles that were introduced in the Docks in Southampton in the early 1920s.

*Standardisation*

By about 1926, all the post-grouping railway companies were experimenting with a kind of container that looked like the body of the standard railway van of the day. It was almost entirely constructed of wood, with metal strapping, had a curved roof, with access doors in the middle of the long sides and usually a door at one end as well. These had many of the features of the modern container, in that the whole thing could be delivered to a customer for packing and unpacking at his convenience and that conveyance could be undertaken by rail, road or sea, or in any combination.

The dimensions of these early units had been standardised by the Railway Clearing House in order that these boxes could be interchanged between systems. The Southern Railway, it was said in the *Shipping Guide* of January 1929, was keeping abreast of the times by introducing new 3.5 ton insulated containers for meat. Apart from the insulation designed to keep food fresh, these were otherwise similar to the standard railway container and were used for the distribution of meat from Southampton. They must have seemed fairly commonplace, as they were described merely as road/rail containers.

In 1931, new Hampshire-made Thornycroft 6 ton model 'JJ' flatbed lorries were introduced that pulled 'Harrow' trailers, and could therefore carry two of these containers on one journey. This new fleet constituted, as the railway company said, 'one of the largest experiments of its kind by any railway company'.

This form of container, with its shaped roof, could not be stacked and the process of slinging them to remove or replace them, and of anchoring down to flat railway wagons with chains, was quite laborious. They persisted through railway nationalisation although never achieved dominance over other forms of freight traffic. British Road Services, which operated 350 general haulage vehicles in its Southampton District as well as fifteen boats plying between Town Quay, Portsmouth and the Isle of Wight, noted in its advertisements in the late 1950s that it used 'special containers' on its services to the Continent and the Isle of Wight. The new cross-Channel cargo ships introduced by British Railways in 1959, the *Elk* and the *Moose*, were also described as having 'ample space for containers and cattle'.

The sort of container described had certain disadvantages and it was only 'standard' in Britain in terms of people having the facilities to handle it. Such containers had gone as far as the United States by sea, for the Southern Railway sent its exhibition stand, the famous Dock Model, to New York in 1939 packed in its own containers. This, however, was exceptional. Towards the end of the Second World War, the United States Army started using a standardised box for supplies, called a 'transporter', but this was only suitable for its own specialist purpose. There was a real need to be able to send goods from shipper to recipient without interference and any intermediate handling had to be with the minimum of fuss.

In the United States, Malcolm McLean, a road haulage operator, is given the credit for devising the concept of the modern rectangular stackable container that he could put on ships to reduce road transport. His containers, first put into operation in April 1956, were 33ft (10.06m) and later 35ft (10.67m) long. Meanwhile, the Matson Shipping Co. had introduced a 24ft (7.32m) container and later Grace Line came up with a 17ft (5.19m) container. It took a further decade for there to be universal agreement on the size, shape and other properties of containers, the International Standards Organisation producing its first standard on container dimensions in January 1968.

## Appearance in Southampton

Meanwhile, in Southampton, these prototypes of the modern container did not take long to appear. In 1959, Lykes Line commenced a service to American ports carrying containers. The US freighter *Ocean Evelyn* loaded 'container traffic' in January 1960, which was flat-topped boxes with a ring in each corner to which chains could be attached and lifted by crane. The Anglo-Overseas Transport Co., a London firm, and its partner the United Cargo Corporation of New York, shipped four of their aluminium containers to South Africa aboard the *Winchester Castle* in April 1960. It was said at the time that this was the first stage in what was hoped would become a round-the-world container service which would eliminate the necessity of shippers having to supply wooden crates.

At the end of 1960 Mr Finnis, Chief Docks Manager for Southampton and Plymouth, gave a paper on handling freight traffic to the Institute of Transport. Afterwards he was asked if containers would provide the answer for the future of freight transport by sea. His reply was that, '… even if changes were introduced in cargo handling, a great deal of work would still be done by traditional methods for many years to come'. On a subsequent occasion he explained this view, as he thought the introduction of containers was in the hands of the shipping companies and they would wish to handle as many types of traffic as possible rather than specialise, while also going to as many different ports as possible. This was a reasonable view for the time, as a great deal of investment was going to be required at every port around the globe in order to provide the facilities to load, unload, manage and store every container that was likely to arrive there.

Nevertheless, the concept was gaining momentum. An article in the September/October 1964 issue of *Docks* magazine was jubilant that the damage sustained to cargo by the old ways of handling would cease and that 'the tyranny of the hook will be brought to an end by the container'. In September 1965, Holland America Line announced that it had decided to start a container ship service to New York in 1967 in conjunction with Wallenius. In late 1965, Overseas Containers Ltd was formed jointly by the P&O Steam Navigation Co., Alfred Holt, British & Commonwealth Shipping and Furness Withy, to 'give concerted study to the development of containerisation and unit loads in ocean liner trades'. Then early in 1966 Associated Container Transportation Ltd was formed by another group of British ship owners comprising Ben Line, Blue Star, Cunard, Ellerman and Harrison Line. Its objective was to 'investigate and promote international container and unit load traffic'. Within a very short time it was announced that Southampton was to become one of the major ports for an experimental Atlantic container service, running containers through from Birmingham to an inland destination in the USA. The sea part of the journey would be on the normal services of Cunard and United States Lines. It began eastbound when the first ship headed for the USA in March carrying fifteen 20ft (6.1m) containers, and it was said that the experiment operated jointly by the National Ports Council in this country and the US Maritime Administration would provide valuable data.

The Managing Director of Ben Line, W.F. Strachan, when speaking to Southampton Chartered Shipbrokers in May 1966, said, 'The Port of Southampton is ideally situated and endowed with land and water resources to take advantage of new shipping developments, particularly the move towards the handling of more and more cargo in containers'. Sir Basil Smallpiece, the Chairman of Cunard, was more direct in not wishing to let an opportunity go by when he said in December 1966, 'In order to catch the new trans-atlantic container ships on their rapid passages to and from Europe, Britain needs a fully-developed container port at Southampton. If we fail, we shall just be bypassed'.

Some of the benefits of containerisation, such as economies of scale and rapid delivery, were beginning to become clear, but only ports with deep water and sufficient space would benefit. London, for example, was going to lose trade.

There was still some confusion as to what container handling really involved in its fully developed form. This goes back to the pioneering work of Malcolm McLean, because initially he was unsure whether he should place the entire wheeled lorry trailer with a container on top in the ship, or just the box part. In Southampton the Swedish Lloyd passenger and cargo service to Bilbao introduced a drive-on drive-off container service in April 1967, operated in conjunction with MacAndrews & Co. Ltd With the 'Macpack' container service, MacAndrews could supply a 20ft (6.1m) container or a 'flat', effectively a container without sides, and the hirer would drop this off at the quayside laden with the cargo. A special 'C'-shaped vehicle that could surround the container and lift it slightly off the ground would then deposit it on the ferry for collection at the end of the voyage. MacAndrews owned some eighty containers and the ship could carry a maximum of twenty-five. Thoresen also purchased a straddle carrier that year to speed container handling on its drive-on drive-off car ferries.

British Rail had gone over to a more conventional 'Railfreight' container at this time, of which Elders & Fyffes were early users. These containers were used to take bananas to Scotland by road rather than rail, which halved the journey time to eighteen hours. The following year Elders & Fyffes were the first to use the new Millbrook Freightliner terminal when it opened on 29 January 1968 and they introduced their own 20ft (6.1m) 'Coldsaver' alloy container a few months later.

While it must have seemed that the British Transport Docks Board was entering into a high-risk project by embarking on the Western Docks Extension Scheme in order to construct a 1,000ft (305m) long deep-water container quay in 1967 before any operator had actually committed to using it, the indications were that containers were the way forward. In fact, the term 'container revolution' first appeared in print at that time.

Stewarts & Lloyds opened a depot in the Western Docks in 1952 for distributing their steel products. The firm also supplied the transport executive with tubular steel stillages as shown here. These forerunners of the modern pallet could be picked up by the Ellwell-Parker electric trucks first introduced by the Southern Railway in 1923. (Bitterne Local History Society)

## The Container Port
In the summer of 1966, Grangemouth Docks, part of the Forth Ports Authority, had become the first fully containerised deep-sea liner service in operation in the country. In June 1967 the British Transport Docks Board published a report that its consultants, McKinsey & Co., had prepared, entitled 'Containerisation: the Key to Low-cost Transport'. It was made freely available to all because of the ramifications to the British economy, and the conclusions were startling.

The report forecast:

- A dramatically rationalised international transport industry consisting of a few large organisations operating throughout the field of transport services
- Fewer shipping lines and ships
- A highly-developed liner train network
- A smaller, but better-rewarded labour force

Containerisation, the report said, could lead to reductions of more than 50 per cent in total transport costs. Less than twenty transoceanic container berths would be needed in Britain on the then present volume of traffic. As a consequence, it was believed that less than one-third of the number of cargo ships then afloat would be required.

There were economies of scale too and the report gave the example of a 2,500 container ship on a 5,000 mile (8,000km) one-way voyage. This would have a unit cost 45 per cent below that of a 300 container ship. This would inevitably lead to concentration of container traffic in the few ports equipped to handle them and an aggregation of UK and continental cargoes.

Manufacturing companies would become more competitive internationally because of reduced transport costs, while promotion of international cooperation would be necessary to facilitate developments.

Britain would benefit because:

- Imports and exports are critical and would cost less
- Being an island, we can capitalise on these major technological developments
- Southampton is the only port in England capable of handling the size of ships likely to be developed without the construction of expensive locks
- At present general cargo can be unloaded at a rate of 20 tons per hatch per hour using twenty-six men. Even allowing for delays, an employee could handle 600 tons of freight in containers in a week compared with thirty currently
- By shifting warehousing, sorting and customs functions away from the Docks and with high-speed loading and unloading of ships, remarkable economies would arise
- There would be higher utilisation of ships with turn-round time cut by 75 per cent.

## Development of Southampton as a Container Port
British Transport Docks Board had purchased 200 acres (81 hectares) of land west of Millbrook Point shortly after the Second World War, so the site was already available for development and government permission to go ahead had been obtained. The contract for the construction of the first part of the Western Docks Extension, the 1,000ft (305m) quay wall, was awarded to Kier Ltd The first bucket of spoil was dredged in February 1967 and the first pile for the crane tracks was driven on 6 June. When the four

phases were complete, it was said that this would form the largest reclamation scheme yet undertaken in Southampton.

Completion of the new quay was rapid. A customs clearance area for 170 containers was formed at the corner of the Western Docks and the new extension. This had an examination shed, administrative block and concrete standing for trailers as well as containers. After two years' use its size had to be doubled because of the demand. Two Paceco-Vickers Portainer cranes, then the largest in the country, were ordered and scheduled for completion on 5 August 1968. One of the first Clark Van Carriers was purchased in order to stack 20ft (6.1m) containers up to three high. Finally, the new quay came into operation with the arrival of Compagnie Maritime Belge's container ship *Teniers*. Although there was no official opening of the quay itself, *Teniers* arrived dressed overall to a civic welcome by the Mayor. The ship discharged thirty containers and loaded thirty on 28 October 1968. The new quay was initially numbered 111 Berth and 112 Berth, following on sequentially from the Western Docks.

*Development of Services*

Compagnie Maritime Belge subsequently joined with Bristol City Line and Clarke Traffic Services of Montreal to form the Dart Containerline Ltd Therefore, by 1970, there were three container groups, all operating to various ports in North America but working out of this common user berth. The first two groups which began using the berth, on 4 December 1969, were Dart and Atlantic Container Line (a consortium formed by Cunard, French Line, Holland America Line, Swedish America Line, Swedish Transatlantic Line and Wallenius). These were followed on 19 December 1969 by Seatrain (UK) Ltd (part of Seatrain Lines incorporated).

Western Docks viewed from 204 Berth in the Container Terminal. (Associated British Ports)

The world's first container services and equipment exhibition was held at Olympia, London, in May 1968. Southampton was represented and models from Olympia showing what the Western Docks Extension would look like and how it would work were exhibited at the Southampton Show that year.

The existing container quay at Southampton was now operating at full capacity, and therefore the British Transport Docks Board applied to the Minister of Transport in early 1970 for approval of the plan to expand the remaining 3,000ft (914m) of quay and hinterland associated with the initial phase of development. This extension of container handling capacity had become necessary in order to meet the demand from other container ship operators, for example Overseas Containers Ltd (OCL) and Associated Container Transportation, who wished to instigate a joint service to the Far East at the end of 1971. Once permission had been obtained for the new development, the work of dredging and land reclamation could begin, and was already underway in July.

The creation of a new access road and separate entrance to this part of the Docks caused the numbering of the new berths to be reconsidered. From December 1970 the existing 111 and 112 Berths were renumbered 201 Berth. Its extension then became 202 Berth. The shorter, angular, corner berth for non-container use would then be 203 Berth and the two berths being created for the Far Eastern service would then become 204 and 205 Berth respectively, with each subsequent 1,000ft (305m) being numbered in sequence. This not only defined the new area, but gave the longer berths required by the ever increasing size of ships. The Portainer crane at 202 Berth was erected in September 1971, with the berth itself coming into operation in January 1972. The remainder of the berths in this phase of development came into operation soon afterwards, 204 Berth in June 1972 and 205 Berth in January 1973.

The Far Eastern service began using 202 Berth until the dedicated space was ready, although the commencement of work was delayed until 1972. In the intervening period the group of shipping companies that intended to operate this service had expanded and was now referred to as Trio Lines. The trio consisted of OCL, Ben Line Containers Ltd (part of ACT), and a new group of European and Far Eastern companies. This last-mentioned group comprised the German company Hapag-Lloyd and the Japanese firms Nippon Yusen Kaisha (NYK) and Mitsui OSK Lines. The first Trio Lines' vessel to inaugurate the service was the *Tokyo Bay*, contributed by OCL. At 58,889 tons she was the largest and fastest container ship in the world at the time and, having arrived on 9 April 1971, set sail on her maiden voyage to Japan two days later. Hapag-Lloyd started its own container services using Southampton in 1983 and, at the end of 1985, a further four new services began. These were Norasia, Holland-Canada, Ben Ocean and Cia Venezolona de Navigacion, the last of which carried Ford Sierra cars in containers to Venezuela. In October 1994 P&O inaugurated the port's first direct container vessel link with the People's Republic of China.

The Maritime Rail Freight Terminal associated with the Western Docks Extension was constructed by Freightliners Ltd and was first used when a ten-wagon train arrived from Manchester at the end of March 1972. This carried containers for shipment on *Kamakura Maru*, part of the Trio service, which had a contract with Freightliners for the inland movement of its containers.

*Tokyo Bay* became the first ship to use 204 Berth when she docked on 8 June, by which time two new Portainer cranes were in use and a third was being erected. *Rhine Maru* of Mitsui OSK was the first ship to use 205 Berth, which came into operation on

4 March 1973 and signalled the completion of this phase of dock development. Traffic was such that the original, though enlarged, bonded container area was completely inadequate and a new, much larger one was built adjacent to the container terminals. While this was being built a temporary area for storing import and export traffic and a vehicle park was created at sheds 107 and 108.

## Further Expansion

By the summer of 1974, a plan for a further extension to the container berths had been submitted to the government by the Dock Board. This would extend from 205 Berth to form another berth (206) and add a further 26 acres (10.5 hectares) to the 98 acres (40 hectares) already brought into use. Its creation was felt necessary if Southampton was to retain the South African trade which was due to be containerised in 1977. In fact, the new berth was not ready until January 1978. The delay was partly owing to a series of industrial disputes concerning pay and working arrangements which were not settled until May. As a consequence, a Trio Lines ship *Kitano Maru* was the first to use 206 Berth on 30 May 1978.

Meanwhile, the vessels operating the South African container service had been obliged to dock in Continental Europe, and the first to come to Southampton was the *City Of Durban*, which arrived in Southampton on 31 May 1978 and tied up at 205 Berth. The South African container service was operated by a consortium of shipping companies, as had become the norm. It was known as the South Africa-Europe Container Service (SAECS) and the companies involved were Ellerman-Harrison Container Line, the owners of *City Of Durban*, OCL, Safmarine, Nedlloyd, P&O Containers, CMB and DAL.

Another consortium, the ACE Group, introduced a Far Eastern service that began on 27 April 1976. This comprised Orient Overseas Container Line (OOCL), Neptune Orient Line, Kawasaki Kisen Kaisha and Franco-Belgian Services. This grouping of shipping lines working together as a consortium was cost effective and, perhaps, inevitable, although it must have added to the complexity of ship operation. Ships and quayside facilities were large and expensive to build and no one company could make the investment in vessels and infrastructure large enough to gain true economies of scale. Taking the example of the South African service, the shipping companies spent £500 million on providing and equipping the vessels, while the South African government spent another £250 million on providing the infrastructure in the ports.

The Container Port in Southampton became known as Prince Charles Container Port from April 1979 when it was announced that His Royal Highness had agreed to the renaming.

Further extension did not take place until the era of Associated British Ports with the building of 207 Berth in 1996. The main channel from Fawley to this new berth was dredged in 1997 and two new super post-Panamax cranes were installed there in 2001.

The Trio consortium broke up in 1991, but its member companies stayed on and three new company groupings were formed at this time linking Southampton to major trade routes. These were: P&O Container Line and Maersk; Hapag-Lloyd, MOL and NYK; and Ben Container Line and Scandutch. After an absence of eleven years, transatlantic container services returned with the arrival of Norasia Line's *Norasia Salome* in 1999. North Atlantic services were further strengthened in 2000 by the coming of the Grand Alliance. This comprised two consortia: P&O Nedlloyd, Hapag-Lloyd, NYK and OOCS; and Lykes Lines and TMM Lines.

Meanwhile, Compagnie Maritime d'Afretment (CMA), which subsequently joined forces with Compagnie General Maritime (CGM), and its partners Norasia Lines and the National Shipping Co. of Saudi Arabia, started a Middle Eastern service in October 1998. Later, in 2001, they formed the North China Express consortium, bringing in the China Shipping Group, Contship and K Line. At approximately the same time, another container shipping group linked Southampton and north China. This was the New World Alliance, which comprised American President Lines (APL), Mitsui OSK and Hyundai Merchant Marine. The first vessel to visit in May 2000 was the 5,300 TEU (Twenty-foot Equivalent Units) *APL Pearl*.

With the growth of this new mode of transport, services sprang up in response to new needs. One of the first to offer facilities to leasing companies and owners for container repair, storage, fumigation, decontamination and painting was A.E. Smith Coggins (Southampton) Ltd operating in conjunction with the shipping firm of Sir William Reardon Smith & Sons. This service began in 1968. Later, in 1971, Containercare (Southern) Ltd created a repair and maintenance facility for containers in West Bay Road. Others have provided similar facilities since.

## Feeder Services

When Cawood's *Craigavon* loaded containers for Belfast in April 1972, a feeder service to Ireland was started. This initiative was followed the same year by other lines aggregating containers for the deep-sea services or in order to distribute imported goods. Currie Line travelled between various Spanish ports and the General Steam Navigation Co. continued its long association with Bordeaux, but this time with containers. A subsidiary of French Line, Rolo Line, started a weekly feeder service in the summer of 1973, linking Southampton, Le Havre and Bilbao. To inaugurate the service, the ship *Ardan* was used, which had a capacity of 95 TEU. Ibesca Container Line joined in, moving between such places as Antwerp and Cadiz, and Bugsier Line commenced container feeder services on 1 February 1974 with the 106 TEU *Teutonia* linking Bremen, Esbjerg, Hamburg and Irish ports. In the first decade of the twenty-first century, some 3 per cent of the throughput of containers is handled this way by transferring from ship to ship. It had previously been a higher percentage, but only because the total number of containers handled has increased.

## Size of Ships

In 1968 it was recorded that the new Atlantic Container Line ships could carry over 800 containers each, a number that seems trivial today. Two years later, on 4 December 1970, one of these ships, *Atlantic Causeway*, was given a civic send-off by the Mayor, Alderman Kathy Johnson, when she was driven on-board over the new link-span bridge at 201 Berth. This was the first of six new second-generation container ships ordered by the company for mixed ro-ro and container carrying. The ship later formed part of the Falklands Task Force to the South Atlantic during the Falklands War of 1982.

The size of ships continued to increase in a repeat of the escalation that had taken place in the Eastern and Western Docks, but this time with container ships. Southampton found itself, as before, well equipped to cope thanks to the investment in infrastructure that had already been made. P&O's *Nedlloyd Stuyvesant* at 984ft (300m) and 80,354 tons was the largest of her kind when she visited in April 2001. She was seventeen containers wide and could carry a total of 6,802 TEU, but by March 2002 Hapag Lloyd's

*Hamburg Express* of 88,493 tons and capable of carrying 7,506 TEU took the record. She was first to be unloaded by the super post-Panamax twin-lift cranes that can handle ships up to twenty containers wide. By comparison, *Kate Maersk* of 6,418 TEU, the first Maersk vessel to return to Southampton in 2006 after an absence of some years, was of only average size. Orient Overseas Container Line named the twelfth of a new series of container ships *OOCL Southampton* in Hong Kong on 28 May 2007. This class of ship are each capable of taking 8,063 TEU.

Ship owners are conservative by nature and did not want to build ships that were too big to pass through the Panama Canal (hence 'Panamax' used as the name of the size and type of crane). Some container ships, however, are now larger than this self-imposed limit. The next marine obstacle that might impede traffic if container ships continue to increase in size is the depth of the Malacca Strait at 69ft (21m). This is greater than the draught of ships that can dock at Southampton, which is 47.5ft (14.5m).

## VOLUME OF TRAFFIC

### Container Traffic

As for the throughput of containers, it is difficult to judge from published figures just how this has changed, except to note that it has increased and increased, dramatically. The *Docks* magazine of July/August 1967 noted an increase from 15,600 in 1965 to 22,000 in 1966, but this was for 'containers and trailers' and really indicates confusion with ro-ro traffic on the Continental ferries as the Container Port had not commenced operations. The number of containers handled by the Container Port when it started in 1968, which was not a full year, was 948. Retrospective figures quoted in a booklet on the Port of Southampton, published in 1982, show the figure rising from 42,402 in 1970 to 364,917 in 1980. Figures from *Docks* magazine (called *Ports Magazine* from 1982) appear lower and may be rounded down, so that the 1990 figure is 336,000, rising to 650,000 in 1995 and 1,000,000 in 2000. By 2008 it was 1.8 million. These are, of course, expressed in TEU or twenty-foot equivalent units (6.1m). Many containers are of the other standard size of 12.2m (40ft), so the number of actual units handled is less than the numbers quoted. The number of containers transferred to and from other ships for delivery has already been noted. Of the remainder, in the 1990s there were some twenty container trains per day which collectively handled one-third of the boxes. Today twenty-five trains a day handle 27 per cent, the remainder going by road on some 2,000 lorries per day.

According to the *Docks* magazine of July/August 1966, Southampton had high hopes of becoming the container capital of the UK. When giving a talk in the city, Sir Arthur Kirby, Chairman of the British Transport Docks Board (BTDB), said he expected Southampton to become a container port for Britain and Northern Europe.

Speaking at the annual dinner of the Southampton Branch of the Institute of Chartered Shipbrokers in 1970, Sir Clifford Dove, CBE, Chairman of the BTDB, said, 'The Port of Southampton, with its first class balance of trade – oil, passengers, general and unit cargo – is set for an extremely bright future'. Referring to the cargo trade, he said that until recently Southampton's general cargo trade, in a national context, was relatively insignificant but bright thinking and the container berth had changed all that.

By 1996 Southampton had become the second largest container port in the UK after Felixtowe. It remains so today.

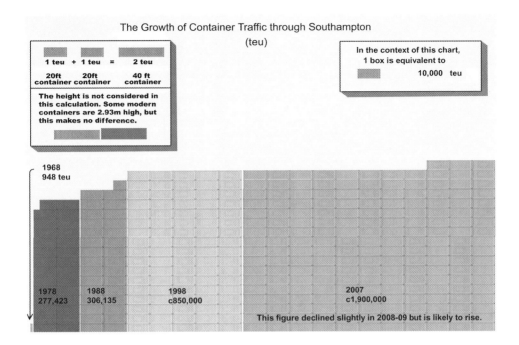

The Growth of Container Traffic through Southampton
(teu)

1 teu + 1 teu = 2 teu

20ft          20ft         40 ft
container container   container

The height is not considered in
this calculation. Some modern
containers are 2.93m high, but
this makes no difference.

In the context of this chart,
1 box is equivalent to

10,000  teu

1968
948 teu

1978          1988                1998                                    2007
277,423    306,135            c850,000                              c1,900,000

This figure declined slightly in 2008-09 but is likely to rise.

## Ownership

In January 1987 a subsidiary company, Southampton Container Terminals Ltd, was set up
by ABP to run Prince Charles Container Port. At the time, Solent Container Services
also existed to provide operational management and systems control. A major change in
working arrangements was agreed with the workforce, which then became permanently
employed on the container berths. A considerable investment in training meant that the
Container Port employees became multi-skilled and flexible. The berths, in order to meet
customer demand, operate twenty-four hours a day, seven days a week.

On 1 July 1988, Southampton Container Terminals merged with Solent Container
Services to form one company and Southampton Container Terminals Ltd itself became
a joint venture company, 49 per cent owned by ABP and 51 per cent owned by shipping companies that were formerly major clients, P&O Containers Ltd and Ben Line. A
major re-equipping programme was immediately put in place, but things did not remain
static on the ownership front. P&O Containers acquired the shares of Ben Line in 1991
and in 1998 the whole of the P&O Containers shares were transferred to P&O Ports
Ltd Then, in 2006, the international container port-owning company DP World bought
P&O Ports and the Admiral Consortium bought ABP. Most recently, in 2008, the name
Southampton Container Terminals was replaced by that of DP World Southampton.

## Speeding up the Process

One of the observations of the BTDB report on the likely impact of containers was
the increased speed of handling goods. Loading and unloading of ships at the quayside
now takes days or even hours compared with the week or more of old. But the speed
of ships themselves was a factor in adopting containers. Some of the early purpose-built
container ships were driven by gas turbines; effectively a power unit like a turbo-prop
aircraft, a form of jet engine. The idea itself was not new. Southampton had been

visited by the first merchant ship to be fitted with gas turbine engines, the tanker *Auris* of Anglo-Saxon Petroleum, on 22 January 1952. Four years later the converted US liberty ship *John Sergeant* also came into the port. Perhaps the first gas-turbine powered container ship to visit Southampton was the *Euroliner* in May 1971. Even at a time when the concept of fuel efficiency was in its infancy, these engines were extravagant. Some ships, like *Liverpool Bay*, were later converted to diesel with a modest loss of speed. Today all container ships are diesel powered, but remain some of the fastest merchant ships afloat.

Much of the success of Southampton as a major container port is due to the development of computerised management systems for handling containers. Southampton has been a leader in the field for many years, with Community Network Services Ltd, a company founded in the restructuring of 1987 but which emerged from the systems department of Solent Container Services, providing the expertise.

All the relevant details of a container and its contents are shared among the interested parties so that HM Revenue & Customs can make any necessary checks and the Port Health Authority is made aware of the nature of foodstuffs. Containers are stacked in advance in the right place to be loaded on the ship in the correct sequence. A system called Radio Data Transfer sends information to a screen in the straddle carrier in order that the driver, whose position is known by GPS, can take the right container to the right place at the time required. At the same time lorries can be scheduled for collection and delivery.

## MAJOR INDUSTRIES

Walter Taylor began his working life as a seaman, where he encountered difficulties with the free running of rope through the wooden blocks. These blocks were essential to the rigging and much else aboard sailing ships, but although the function of each block was pretty much the same wherever they were used, each unit had to be carved by hand. On his return to shore, Taylor and his son (also Walter) endeavoured to find a solution. Their answer to the problem was to mechanise the process, so that each block could be made quickly and to the same pattern as its fellows. The processes involved in manufacture were only part-mechanised, but meant that Walter had to adapt the circular saw for use as an industrial tool. The Taylors' first specimen was submitted to the Board of Ordnance in 1759 and as a result they were offered a contract to supply all the gun tackle blocks to the Navy. Rigging blocks were also submitted to the Admiralty for approval with the encouragement of the local MP, Hans Stanley. These too were accepted and Walter Taylor Jnr went into production in 1762, just after his father's death.

The Taylors' processes were further developed by Marc Brunel, father of Isambard, who offered to share his improved machinery but was refused. Walter Taylor's business, though successful, was dissolved after his death in 1803.

The Taylors' firm had originally been established in Westgate Street, but they had to move first to Weston and then to Woodmill, where a waterwheel on the Itchen provided power to drive the machinery.

This lack of available power within the town has been put forward as an explanation for the lack of early industry in Southampton before the age of steam. The problem can also, in part, be laid at the feet of the merchant guild who did what they could to stifle any development that might be seen as a distraction from their main business of trade. Later, Mudie wrote that 'at least until times comparatively recent', Southampton was 'a mere place of transit'.

In the modern docks, General Motors created an assembly plant for cars and commercial vehicles at the western end of the New Docks, which began operations in the autumn of 1938. The plant covered 240,000 sq. ft (22,320 sq. m) and employed 300 people assembling components supplied directly from the United States. At the outbreak of the Second World War the factory went over to the production of vehicles for the Canadian government, but was severely damaged in a bombing raid in November 1940 and work moved to the north of England. The company returned in November 1946 and spent two years reconditioning Army vehicles. A parts department was re-established and a diesel engine reconditioning department developed using 49,000 sq. ft (4,560 sq. m) that had been rebuilt after the war. By mid-1951, a further 122,000 sq. ft (11,350 sq. m) had come into use.

By October 1950, the main portion of the factory was occupied by the A.C. Sphinx Spark Plug Co., a subsidiary of General Motors. While the main factory was in Dunstable, special purpose machine tools were being installed at the Southampton plant for the production of a new type of oil filter for use with modern petrol engines. This was the disposable cartridge filter with which modern drivers are so familiar, although the role of Southampton in its development and introduction is less well known. The *Shipping Guide* of June 1951 noted that it was expected that within a short period, thousands would be produced daily and that while 150 people were currently employed, within six months this would rise to 600, twice the original workforce. In fact, by the end of 1956 the factory covered 6 acres (2.4 hectares) and employed 1,000 people, the name of the division having been changed in 1954 to A.C. Delco. While the cartridge filter was a great success and revolutionised the way engines are maintained, it was soon manufactured by others; Purolator claimed to have invented it in the United States in 1955, and cheaper sources of manufacture developed. The Southampton factory could not compete and eventually closed in 1998.

## Ford Transit

An aircraft factory had been established near Southampton Airport by Sir Hugo Cunliffe-Owen in 1937, but while it prospered for a while during the Second World War with the assembly of American fighters, it was never a great success. Part of the site was occupied by Briggs Motor Bodies Ltd in 1953, the company having become a subsidiary of Ford that year, and body panels for Ford Thames vans were pressed out here. At one time, Ford factories in different countries produced designs intended for local consumption, but in the early 1960s a European Division was created. The Ford Transit van was an early product of this reorganisation, replacing a predecessor vehicle produced only in Germany. This revolutionary light goods vehicle appeared in 1965, although the body panels were shipped from Southampton to be assembled in Langley, Berkshire, and also in Ghent in Belgium. In 1972 the assembly line was moved to Southampton and production of the whole vehicle started in July. Since then it has gone through six major updates and the current model is also made in Mexico, but the bulk of the 5 million produced so far have been made in Southampton and a considerable number have been exported from the port.

## Cable Manufacture

Almost adjacent to and south-east of the General Motors plant, between West Bay Road and Herbert Walker Avenue, Standard Telephones & Cables Ltd began construction of a factory for the manufacture of submarine telephone cable and submerged repeaters. Construction of this establishment, which commenced in 1954, was reputed to cost £1 million and covered approximately 10 acres (4 hectares). The new factory, it was said, would be the equal of any in the world. The first shipment of cable was delivered, via an overhead gantry across Herbert Walker Avenue, directly into the hold of the waiting cable ship *Ijsel* on 17 November 1956, although the factory itself was not completed until the following spring. Large orders were received from the outset. The factory began by producing the traditional type of armoured cable, but the building of an extension to the west began in October 1959.

The new unit, which opened in 1963, was referred to as the No.2 Factory and produced lightweight armour-less submarine cable developed by Bell Telephone Laboratories in the United States. The two elements of the Southampton factory together had the largest manufacturing capacity for submarine telephone cable in the world. As the result of a merger in 1970, Standard Telephones & Cables became the only manufacturer of submarine telephone cable in the country and one of only four in the world. The plant in Western Docks became the UK headquarters of the submarine division. By 1975 it was making 70 per cent of the world's total requirements, producing some 3,000 miles (4,800km) per year. Landward storage was provided for 6,200 miles (10,000 km) of cable.

The development of optical fibre began in 1978 and production started in 1986 with the making of the material for the first international system, the link between Britain and Belgium. Confidence in the success of their new product was echoed in the company's advertisements, which identified them as 'the light at the bottom of the ocean'.

The company diversified to the manufacture of tubing for land drains in 1965, using the brand name 'Pipaway'. STC ceased to exist in 1991.

Pirelli General had begun manufacturing electrical cable in Southampton just before the First World War in their factory in Western Esplanade. This was initially rubber and fabric-covered material for domestic and industrial applications, lifts, etc., with some armoured cable being produced from the 1920s. A separate factory was set up to manufacture submarine power cables in West Quay Road, with work starting on the building in 1983. It was specifically constructed to manufacture the power cables linking Britain and France, and had a similar gantry arrangement to that of Standard Telephones & Cables, but crossing West Quay Road to go to 101 Berth.

Cable ships receiving material from STC had docked at the western end of the Western Docks, where the largest of this type of vessel could be accommodated. With the creation of the first part of the Western Docks Extension, the Post Office Telecommunications Division decided to site its cable ship depot on 2.5 hectares of reclaimed land at 203 Berth where the quay wall turns through 270 degrees. Not only were there the usual advantages of the port, but there was easy and rapid access to the main areas of their work in the Channel, Western Approaches and North Sea. Work commenced in March 1973 and it was officially opened on 20 November 1974 by Mr G. MacKenzie MP, Under Secretary of State for Industry.

New cable ships were commissioned to maintain Britain's 15,000 miles (24,000km) of undersea cable. *Monarch* was launched on 29 January 1975 by Lady Ryland, wife of the Chairman of the Post Office, and *Iris* was launched later the same year. These ships, together with *Alert*, the largest vessel in the fleet which was devoted to cable laying rather than repair, were designed to be loaded by a revolutionary high-speed technique. Steel cylinders, or 'pans', 18ft (5.5m) in diameter, 12ft (3.7m) high and ready-filled with the correct material, were moved alongside a cable ship with ease using an air cushion and craned aboard. This was not only very much quicker than the previous method employed, but avoided the potential for damage to a large extent.

Cable & Wireless (Marine) Ltd acquired the business and facilities of BT Marine, as it had become, in 1994, thus becoming the world's largest submarine installation and maintenance contractor. *Edward Wilshaw* had been the first Cable & Wireless ship to visit the Docks in February 1958, taking cable for Gibraltar, so their presence was not new. However, the Cable & Wireless fleet was sold and the operating base moved to Portland in Dorset in 1999.

## Oil Refining

In 1921 a small oil refinery was built at Fawley by the Agwi Petroleum Corporation Ltd, which later became part of Esso. This was unusual because Britain had generally imported refined oil products, mostly from the United States, and this continued to be the case until after the Second World War. It was, however, an ideal site for expansion and for siting one of the new plants that would refine crude oil, mainly from the Middle East, in order to make Britain independent of other supplies of refined products.

The present Fawley refinery was the first and largest of these new post-war facilities and was built using imported plant and equipment. The first shipment of the 100,000 tons of machinery needed for the plant arrived in Southampton on 22 September 1949. The plant was opened by the then Prime Minister, Clement Attlee, just over two years later and a few months ahead of schedule, on 14 November 1951. At the time it was the largest refinery in Europe and sixth largest in the world. Fawley's position was and is ideal for distribution of the refined products to a wide area and for the reception of the world's largest tankers, although the jetty was not completed when the Prime Minister opened it. This marine jetty is approximately a mile long and is built over Southampton Water on concrete piles. On the outside there are five berths for the large crude carriers to discharge, and on the inside there are four berths for smaller coastal tankers to distribute the finished products. The refinery remains one of the most modern in Europe and processes 16.5 million tons of crude oil per year.

While Fawley Refinery was conceived to accept the largest tankers, it is doubtful if anyone imagined just how large they would become. In 1950, a large tanker was 26,000 tons. In 1957, the Harbour Board approved a dredging scheme promoted by Esso Petroleum Co. to enable tankers of 65,000 tons to be dealt with at the Marine Terminal. By 1970, tankers had grown to 90,000 tons, and each new generation has been bigger still. For example, the *Esso Kawasaki* of 1975 was 302,576 d.w. tons; *Wind Escort* of 1980 was 357,632 d.w. tons; and the *Burmah Endeavour* of 1984 was 450,000 d.w. tons.

Three petrochemical works were established downstream of the refinery – those of Monsanto Chemicals, Union Carbide and International Synthetic Rubber. When built in 1960, the butyl rubber plant was the first in Britain and only the fifth in the world. The entire complex, including the refinery, has been part of ExxonMobil since 1999.

On the other side of Southampton Water is the Hamble Oil Terminal of BP. This was established in 1925 as their distribution centre for the south of England. In 1990, it became the sole export point for the crude oil produced from the Wytch Farm oilfield in Dorset.

## Tobacco

From 1913, British American Tobacco (BAT) had a small factory in Blechynden Terrace by the main railway line from London to Bournemouth, near the present railway station. Their second plant in Southampton was the Millbrook factory, opened in 1923. 'M' warehouse in the Docks was the bonded warehouse for the dried tobacco leaf that had been brought in from overseas. Cunard and White Star had brought small consignments, but a regular import trade was not established until Anchor-Brocklebank started bringing Virginian tobacco to Southampton, beginning with the arrival of *Malakuta* on 17 October 1930. Additional warehousing was provided in 1935, but it was not until late 1960 that a replacement for the bombed 'D' warehouse was provided, where the ground floor was used for sherry and the first floor for raw tobacco. Post-war supplies were imported from India and South Africa for BAT by P&O and Clan Line. The finished product in the form of cigarettes was re-exported to India and the Far East, mainly on P&O ships. BAT closed its manufacturing plant in Southampton in 2006.

## Beer, Wine and Spirits

Wine was one of the principal commodities imported to Southampton in medieval times but the trade had declined to virtually nothing by the beginning of the seventeenth century. The nineteenth century saw a renewal of the flow of wine coming through the port. Southampton had already become the entrepôt for the liqueur Grande Chartreuse by 1900.

Vessels of the General Steam Navigation Co. had been occasional visitors to Southampton since 1842, but regular services every ten days from Bordeaux were established in March 1893, principally to act as a feeder coinciding with the arrival of American Line. Although it brought other commodities in season, it was noted for the import of wine. The fortnightly service from Tonnay-Charente was locally and informally known as the 'brandy boat'.

South African wine had commanded high prices in Europe in the eighteenth and nineteenth centuries, but the trade had been supported by a preferential duty which was withdrawn in 1861. A cooperative known as KWV was set up by Cape wine farmers in 1919 to recapture the ailing European markets, particularly in Britain. Its main depot, which opened in 1931, was operated by a subsidiary, South African Wine Farmers' Association (London) Ltd, and was at the railway depot at Nine Elms in London. This proved unequal to the task as imports increased, and the association looked for a location in which to expand. Southampton seemed the natural choice as mail steamers already had regular links with the port, land was available and landward communications were good. A purpose-built bonded warehouse, 'W' bond, at 106 Berth Western Docks was erected for the South African Wine Farmers' Association. It had bulk storage of the most modern kind in Europe, and was first put into use when *Southampton Castle* made the first bulk delivery of 60,000 gallons of wine from her purpose-built glass-lined tanks on 9 July 1965. The depot also had a rail connection, a cooperage and a garage for the road tankers, and by 1960 about 50 per cent, or 700,000 gallons (3.1 million litres), of South African wine was passing through Southampton each year. In 1963 an experiment was made with bulk handling in 500 gallon (2,300 litres) tanks, a sort of early container.

In the early years the wine was discharged into articulated road tankers, which then offloaded their contents into tanks at the depot, but it was connected by stainless steel pipes to the dockside by means of pumps and a gantry over Herbert Walker Avenue in 1977. From the early 1970s, the enterprise was operated by a subsidiary company, the Southampton Warehousing Co., which also imported South African sherry and wine in bulk from Sicily.

The original site of 4 acres (1.6 hectares) was extended in 1967, nearly doubling its capacity to 1 million gallons (4.5 million litres) and again in 1973, making it capable of holding 1.5 million gallons (6.8 million litres).

Bulk wine handling was further enhanced by the construction of a warehouse and bottling plant for Martini & Rossi Ltd on a 1 hectare site on the south side of West Bay Road by 106 and 107 Berths. This, the company's sole UK import centre, opened in early 1976 and comprised bottling lines capable of supplying and storing 3 million cases of wine per year. By the end of 1989, additional outside storage tanks and two more bottling lines were in use. Martini was acquired by Bacardi in 1992 and Cypress sherry and Bacardi rum were added to the product mix. Ten years later, in 2002, 2.1 million gallons (9.5 million litres) were imported and bottled at Southampton.

Typically there were ten shipments of vermouth from Italy and six shipments of rum from Trinidad and the Bahamas received per year at the Docks in dedicated wine tank ships. The method had already been established in 1973 when the *Astree* discharged 388,000 gallons (1.76 million litres) of wine from Palermo on 24 July, while the South African Wine Farmers' Association chartered the *Maguelone* to bring their wine to Southampton on 11 October 1974.

The need for economies of scale and enhanced competition caused the Bacardi Martini plant to close in the summer of 2007.

To meet the needs of ships' crews and those of passengers travelling on ships from Southampton, various specialist exporters and bonded warehousemen have been established at the port. One such was Edward Young & Co. which flourished in the 1920s, although perhaps the most well known was C.G. Hibbert & Co. Ltd, which was founded in London in 1763 and which established premises in Southampton in 1901. Hibberts supplied companies such as Union Castle and are remembered for providing the beer consumed on the *Titanic*.

As the Docks were reconstructed after the Second World War, Hibberts began construction of a new store and bottling plant in Western Docks, although they kept the old bonded warehouse that had survived the Blitz. The new building opened in August 1950 but was soon found to be too small. Work started on an extension in October 1952, which was opened by Major Hibbert on 3 July 1954.

The opening ceremony was significant in two ways. Miss Valerie Glass, a descendant of the first Governor of Tristan da Cunha, unveiled a plaque commemorating the crew who had survived the wreck of the *Blendenhall* on Inaccessible Island in 1821. The shipwrecked mariners had survived their three-month ordeal before being rescued by eating penguin meat and drinking Hibbert's Porter. The second thing was of more historical significance, for Hibberts unveiled to the public the first beers in Britain to be packed in flat-topped cans, which had been developed in conjunction with the Metal Box Co. Beer had been packed in tins in the 1930s, but these had been in the form of the 'Brasso' type tin with a conical top and a screw cap, which actually provided very little advantage over glass bottles. The company's advertisement in shipping literature of 1954 proclaimed 'We've done it!', and went on to say that the new flat-topped can was cheaper, saved space and weight, and that the beer kept longer. So Hibberts became first in the field and from then on the lines in the bonded store produced canned as well as bottled beer.

An associate company of C.G. Hibbert, Solent Wine & Spirit Co. Ltd, took over an existing warehouse adjacent to Hibberts in Solent Road. This became 'U' bond and opened on 13 June 1962. It too had a claim to fame, being at the time the largest bonded ships' store in the country. Towards the end of 1972, C.G. Hibbert & Co. Ltd merged with Sealine Services (Marine Supplies) Ltd, and C.G. Hibbert became the wine and spirit division.

C.G. Hibbert & Co. still exists in Dover, although the company severed its connection with Southampton in the 1980s.

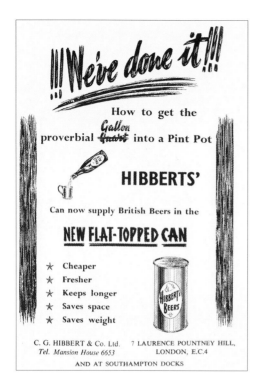

Hibbert's triumphant announcement of 1954 that the firm had created a new and improved way of packaging beer, in conjunction with the Metal Box Co. (C.G. Hibbert & Co. Ltd)

## Ship Maintenance and Repair

The provision of facilities like dry docks was considered an essential feature of the port when there was a large, locally-based fleet and the dry docks themselves, including their creation and adaptation to changing circumstances, have been described earlier. They were considered to be part of the infrastructure of the Docks and, while owned by respective dock companies or the State, were leased to operators who provided the service.

The pioneering steamship companies using Southampton had initially to dry dock in Portsmouth or even London before local facilities were created. The Royal Mail Steam Packet Co. established a 'factory' in the Docks to cater for its own needs as no existing facilities were on hand, but even before that had a floating works in the form of the hulk of the *North Britain*. This was able to turn out iron boilers for the entire fleet as required during the 1840s and 1850s. The original 'factory' was sited to the east of the sugar refinery at the extremity of the Docks. Later it was re-sited at the former lairage in Test Road, which was acquired in 1923. That building, dating from 1900, was destroyed by fire in 1936, rebuilt the following year and destroyed again, this time by bombing, in November 1940. New stores, workshops and offices were rebuilt on the site in 1954. A speciality product of the workshops were 5ft (1.5m) diameter rod fenders (compact bundles of wooden staves bound with rope) carried on the ships and used in South American ports.

All the major vessels of the White Star Line were built in Belfast by Harland & Wolff and the company naturally wanted its shipbuilder to handle repairs when it established its principal services in Southampton. Harland & Wolff obligingly established a repair facility at Trafalgar Dry Dock in 1907 and this facility was almost immediately put to the test when the *Suevic* ran aground on the Manacles Rock on 17 March 1907. To save the ship, she was cut in half, the stern part towed to Southampton and a new bows section

*Above:* The Royal Mail Co.'s depot at the Lairage shows the view across Empress Dock towards the Itchen, not long after the railway grouping. It was unusual for Union Castle ships to use the Empress Dock, but *Kenilworth Castle*'s name is clearly visible between the depot buildings. (Stan Roberts)

*Left:* Harland & Wolff advertisement of the 1930s. The company established a repair depot in Southampton in 1907, which remained in operation until 1973. (Private collection)

fabricated in Belfast. The two parts were then successfully united in Southampton and *Suevic* steamed on uneventfully before being sold in 1928.

The firm of J.I. Thornycroft & Co. Ltd began the process of relocating its shipbuilding works from Chiswick to Woolston in 1904. During the First World War, ship repair became a major part of its activities with 1.2 million tons of merchant shipping passing through its hands for repair, mainly owing to war damage. The long-established shipbuilding enterprise of Day, Summers in Northam was also heavily engaged in ship repair during the First World War, handling 369 vessels on its slipways – mostly patrol vessels, 'P' boats, torpedo boats and trawlers.

While Day, Summers, a once enterprising and innovative firm, continued to decline, its last advertisement appearing in November 1928, others were in the ascendancy. J. Samuel White & Co. Ltd, shipbuilders from the Isle of Wight, established a ship repair depot near Prince of Wales Dry Dock in 1923. Husband's repair facility was established in Marchwood in the early 1920s and became a limited company, Husbands Shipyards Ltd, in 1938, with its own tugs, deep water berth and slipways and, at one time, a floating crane. The British Arc Welding Co. Ltd, which had been established in London in 1910, set up a large depot in Southampton before the First World War, its processes having been sanctioned by the Board of Trade for the repair of boilers.

By the late 1930s there were three major ship repairers in Southampton: Harland & Wolff, J.I. Thornycroft and the Southern Railway. Each had specific clients among the shipping companies. Harland & Wolff began as repairers to White Star, but expanded to include Royal Mail and its associated companies, Union Castle and some Cunard vessels. The Southern Railway Co. maintained its own fleet which, by the time of nationalisation, consisted of forty vessels from along the South Coast. J.I. Thornycroft had handled the bulk of Cunard work from its arrival in Southampton, its advertisements proclaiming it to be 'official contractors … to the Cunard Steam Ship Company', with a period when it was termed 'official repairers to Cunard White Star'. Thornycroft also maintained the Royal Research Ships, the Red Funnel fleet and troop ships. With the coming of the Floating Dock, Thornycroft could state that it could handle the 'smallest of vessels to the world's largest liners', and in fact handled what was probably the largest ship reconstruction project ever undertaken in Southampton when the shell of the Furness Withy ship *Monarch Of Bermuda*, which had been burned out, arrived in March 1947 to be reconstructed. It reappeared in 1950 as the Australian emigrant ship *New Australia*.

During the Second World War, some of the dry dock facilities were taken over for a period with preparations for the invasion of Europe and the construction of major Mulberry Harbour parts. Nevertheless, Harland & Wolff handled repairs to an astonishing 7,250 vessels of all types, although only 550 of these required dry docking.

On the strength of its ship repair facilities, the status of Southampton, as judged by the Committee of Lloyd's Register of Shipping, was raised in January 1951 from that of a Senior Port to being a Principal Port.

Both Harland & Wolff and J.I. Thornycroft had floating workshops at this time, the Thornycroft vessel being named *Lightwell*. *Harlandic II* of Harland & Wolff was particularly useful when servicing large tankers at Fawley or the Hamble. These craft had facilities to support welding operations and to supply electricity and compressed air although, in late 1959, the Dock owners provided compressed air installations at both 25 Berth and 45 Berth with underground pipes so that ship repairers had power available without the necessity of cluttering the quayside with compressors.

In 1966, Thornycroft and Vospers of Portsmouth merged to form Vosper Thornycroft. Then in the summer of 1973, Harland & Wolff announced that its Southampton ship repair establishment was to be sold. As has been noted elsewhere, ship repair is highly seasonal in character and the company had diversified in the late 1950s to manufacturing barges and fabricating steelwork for buildings in order to retain its workforce. Vosper Thornycroft too had used its fitting-out skills to create, amongst other things, interiors for public houses, and it was Vosper Thornycroft that took over the Harland & Wolff business. This company itself underwent a period of nationalisation, forming a division of British Shipbuilders from the mid-1970s until a management buyout of late 1985 returned it to private ownership. The firm was hard hit a decade later by a further recession in the shipping industry, when overcapacity and a decline in orders, coupled with competition from state-subsidised rivals overseas, led to the closure of the ship repair division in 1987.

Apart from Husbands, this left the Thew Engineering Group, which had been established in 1970, as the major ship repairer. Only about half of its business was connected with ship repair and the diversity of its operations was thought to even out market fluctuations. Initially the firm had covered repair and building slipways upriver in Woolston and later undertook work in the larger dry docks. The marine part of the business was taken over by A. & P. (Southampton) Ltd, a subsidiary of the A. & P. Group, in 1989. Although a newcomer to Southampton, this company had at the time nearly fifty years' experience in the field and styled itself as 'Europe's leading ship repairer'. It established its base at King George V Dry Dock and transformed the area into a thriving ship repair base. In the late twentieth century, A. & P. overhauled such large and famous ships as *Canberra*, *Oriana*, *Norway*, *Black Prince*, *Black Watch* and completed a refit of the *Queen Elizabeth 2* in the spring of 1997. The firm left Southampton in 2005 owing to a shortage of work and King George V Dry Dock, then the only remaining dry dock in Southampton, closed in 2006. The facility at Husbands former yard in Marchwood has, since 2002, been operated by Central Ship Repairers (UK) Ltd

Otherwise, there have been some notable achievements in ship maintenance and repair that have taken place in Southampton. In the post-war conversion of *Queen Mary* and *Queen Elizabeth* from troop ships to passenger carrying in 1946-47, an army of workers was required and 1,500 people were brought down from Glasgow. The extra numbers put pressure on the existing catering arrangements, and so the entire shed at 101 Berth was converted into a canteen so the additional workers could be fed. In 1950 the *Empire Windrush*, herself a former Hamburg Sud liner and later a British troop ship, was modernised and used briefly as an immigrant ship, and another similar craft, *Empire Orwell*, was fitted out as a pilgrim ship for the Pan-Islamic Steamship Co. in 1958, running to and from Jeddah.

Much of the refitting of the *Queen Elizabeth 2* took place at various times in Southampton. In October 1972 she was fitted with two new blocks of ten luxury penthouse suites fabricated from aluminium on the quayside at 40 Berth by Vosper Thornycroft Ltd and placed on the port and starboard sides of the ship by floating crane. In all, fifty new cabins were added at this time and the kitchens and restaurants reconstructed in a £1.75 million 'face-lift' programme. Thornycroft also fitted stabilisers to both *Queen Elizabeth* and *Queen Mary* in Southampton in January 1955 and February-March 1957 respectively. This was at a time when older vessels were being retro-fitted with these stabilisers which gave passengers a much more comfortable voyage in rough seas. It should be noted that the very first Denny-Brown stabilisers were fitted new to the Southern Railway cross-Channel steamer *Isle of Sark* by her builders in 1932.

Husbands fitted out an oil drilling rig for exploratory work in Lulworth Cove in October 1963. Another, the *Gulf Tide*, came from the Irish Sea for an overhaul in early 1970, as did the *North Star*. The work on both of these was carried out by Vosper Thornycroft. The most significant development to take place in this field, however, was the construction of an oil rig in Southampton. In late 1957, Steel Structures Ltd acquired the 'blue lagoon', a reclaimed area to the west of King George V Dry Dock that had up to that time only been used as an ash tip. When the first plate was cut in February 1958, it was the beginning of the first ever oil rig to be built in Britain and only the fifteenth in the world. It was launched on 13 October that year and named *Orient Explorer* by Mrs Mary Carberry, the wife of the Works Manager. The rig was for use by the Brunei Shell Petroleum Co. Ltd in North Borneo and, with legs that could extend 150ft below the surface of the sea, was the greatest depth then achieved by a mobile platform. It used an American invention, the de Long jack, to extend and retract the legs and incorporated a helicopter landing platform. A second similar platform was proposed in March 1959, but the prediction by the *Shipping Guide* that this new phenomenon of searching for and extracting oil from beneath the sea 'may well herald the establishment of a new industry' proved unfounded, at least for Southampton. The journal was however correct in stating that 'underwater drilling will become commonplace'.

## Shipbuilding

Recent underwater archaeological investigation at Bouldnor Cliff, off Yarmouth on the Isle of Wight, has revealed a specialised industrial site that may be a Mesolithic boatyard. If this proves to be correct, then shipbuilding is older than any other local activity described in this book.

Shipbuilding to supply local needs had long been practiced in Southampton, although Naval vessels were also built when required. The ships of Henry V's navy were mainly built in Southampton or at Deptford, one of the largest being the *Grace Dieu* of approximately 1,500 tons. The *Anne*, launched in Southampton in 1416, is perhaps the most technologically interesting, for she was the first ship with two masts recorded as having been built in England. Behind the main mast, which was square-rigged, she had another carrying a fore and aft sail for manoeuvrability. This development had first appeared in carracks in the Mediterranean about sixty years previously, and the concept gradually spread northwards.

The construction of Henry VII's dry dock in Portsmouth in 1495 created the split between military and merchant shipping, with Portsmouth focusing on the Navy and Southampton concentrating on merchant activity. Warships, however, continued to be built in Southampton – the eighty-gun *Cornwall* of 1692 and the forty-six-gun *Mediator* of 1782 being just two examples.

The first modern shipyard was established by Day, Summers in 1840, the firm having moved from the site it had occupied in Foundry Lane, Millbrook, since 1834, to a more convenient location on the banks of the Itchen in Northam. Early iron steamships were built together with their propelling machinery for Royal Mail SP Co. (the *Nile*) in 1864, Hamburg America Line (the *Allemania*) in 1865 and P&O (the *Hindostan*) in 1869 until restrictions on the size of the ships that could be built on the river caused shipping companies to go further afield for passenger vessels. One of Day, Summers' last products in 1928 was the tug *Kenneth*. In better days, the firm had rectified the *Great Eastern* in May 1860 before her first commercial voyage, though not in its yard.

On the opposite bank of the Itchen, at Woolston, a yard was started by Oswald, Mordaunt in 1876. While not financially successful, many robust and elegant sailing ships were built there. There were also unusual products such as an early tanker, and *Solent*, the first Royal Mail paddle steamer to be used for cruising in the Caribbean, was built by the firm in 1878. When Mordaunt moved in 1889, and following a brief period of inactivity, the yard was run by the Southampton Naval Iron Works until 1893. After this the yacht building firms of J.G. Fay and Mordey, Carney & Co. Ltd jointly operated from the yard until it was taken over by J.I. Thornycroft in 1904. The firm settled on this as a more useful site than Chiswick for the larger vessels then required. Many high-speed Naval craft were constructed, particularly during both World Wars, and in the First World War submarine diesel engines were built, as was the well-known decoy or 'Q' ship *Hyderabad*. During the First World War the firm had 'Engaged in War work which included the building of 43 war vessels, 5,000 motor lorries [at Basingstoke] and over 100 motor boats, also depth charge throwers and other munitions'.

By 1920, 'output of marine engine horse-power at Southampton totalled 196,250 IHP. More than double the next largest builder in the country'.

Thornycroft survived the depression of the 1920s by engaging in Naval work and in building steam and motor yachts for wealthy clients. The firm continued to innovate and constructed the world's first warship with a glass-fibre hull, the minesweeper HMS *Wilton*, in 1972. As has been noted elsewhere, the firm combined its activities with Vosper of Gosport, and after a period of nationalisation continued independently on the site until 2003. The last craft to go down the slipway was the yacht *Mirabella V*, though at 303.5ft (92.5m) she was as big as many warships.

While builders such as Thornycroft had produced high-speed craft since the beginning of the twentieth century, mention must be made of the British Power Boat Co. which was started in Hythe in September 1927 by Hubert Scott-Paine. Having started Supermarine Aviation with Noel Pemberton-Billing and gone on to be a founding director of Imperial Airways, he turned his love of fast boats to account by designing and building them. These attracted the interest of the Air Ministry in 1931 and his company received its first order for torpedo boats from the Admiralty in 1933. The firm went on to produce a range of specialist craft, including rescue launches and target towing boats during the Second World War, but closed in 1946 having outgrown its need.

Many notable people have passed through Southampton and while most leave no trace, the artist J.M. Whistler was moved to create this etching in July 1887 which he entitled 'Dry Dock, Southampton'. In fact, it depicts the shipyard of Oswald, Mordaunt, a firm that used a dock for the construction of vessels rather than a slipway. (University of Glasgow, Hunterian Museum & Art Gallery)

*Labour*

Dock workers throughout the country were traditionally casually employed, and were obliged to present themselves twice a day in the hope of being selected by a foreman to undertake loading and unloading duties. Men who were not selected did not work and therefore earned no money. During the Second World War, Ernest Bevin introduced a registration scheme for dock workers. The post-war government incorporated this idea into its National Dock Labour Scheme in 1947 in response to the dock strike of 1945. The principal objective of the scheme was to 'decasualise' dock work; in other words, to give the dock worker a legal right to security of employment, holidays, sick pay and a pension. The scheme was responsible for the dockers' registration, allocation of his work, payment, training and medical care. It was administered by the National Dock Labour Board, through local committees, and consisted of representatives from the employers and trade unions in equal number.

The new Dock Labour Scheme did not, at first, entirely do away with the custom of being 'called'. In Southampton, in the post-war era at least, dockers gathered to be 'called' or selected at Shed 101 in the New Docks or at the old Employment Exchange building in Albert Road, in relative proximity to the Old Docks. A new National Dock Labour Board centre was created in Lower Canal Walk in 1952 and started work in January, but was not officially opened until 26 February. The flat-roofed building of sand-coloured brick contained offices, a board room, a rest area where those who had not been allocated work could wait for the next 'call', and a massive 'call stand'. In this hall, 1,000 men could await work allocation by Port Labour Officers in the morning and again in the afternoon before clocking in. Southampton was the first to have this specialist facility and it was hoped at the time that it would be a model for other ports.

Decasualisation of dock labour began on 18 September 1967. From that date the registered dock worker, although he was still employed by the National Dock Labour Board, was allocated, permanently where possible, to a licensed port employer rather than having to go through the process of being 'called'.

In Southampton, where the transition went more smoothly than in other places, there was a further step which came into effect on 1 January 1968, where the dock worker was allocated to a new licensed employer, the Southampton Cargo Handling Co. Ltd This was a company formed jointly by the British Transport Docks Board and the South Coast Stevedoring Co. Ltd

There had been some independent stevedores in the Docks for many years and the South Coast Stevedoring Co. was itself formed in 1966 by the amalgamation of the firm of J. Rose & Co. Ltd which was founded in 1898, and the London & Southampton Stevedoring Co. Ltd, established in 1959 to handle Union Castle operations in the Docks.

In 1969 the National Ports Council attributed the diminishing number of days lost through disputes directly to the introduction of decasualisation, and Southampton's industrial relations were the best of all the UK ports with an average of only half a day lost per docker per year. Then in 1973, the Southampton Cargo Handling Co. merged with British Transport Docks Board, making BTDB again the sole licensed employer of the dock workers.

Following its original aims, the National Dock Labour Board opened a new Port Medical Centre near Dock Gate 2 in the Old Docks on 12 December 1949. It was staffed by two nurses and later had a part-time medical officer. This was followed by a similar facility near 105 Berth in the New Docks, opened by the Mayor on 8 January 1951. This

was the first building in Southampton Docks to be designed by the BTDB's own architect. A new NDLB Sports, Social and Welfare Club was later provided in Eastgate Street,
and was opened on 2 November 1970 by the Chairman, Mr P.G.H. Lewison.

A Training School for dockers was established by the National Dock Labour Board in
1965, on the south side of Inner Dock at 14 Berth, in premises that had formerly been used
by the Solent Division of the Royal Naval Reserve. The following year, the school acquired
an outdoor area with masts, derricks and dummy cargo with which the trainees could practice. In late 1970, the first training course for instructors in dock work was instituted there.
A year before, however, another training area had been set up at the back of the new container berth which offered week-long courses in the stowage and lashing of containers and
other cutting edge skills connected with securing cargo on trailers inside ro-ro ships. All the
containers and equipment for this scheme, the first such course in the country, were supplied by the consortia using the port, Dart and Atlantic Container Lines, and demonstrated
the commitment to proper training for what has always been an extremely dangerous job.

The National Dock Labour Scheme, while formed with good intentions, was need-
lessly bureaucratic in operation and not adaptable to change. Employers believed that it
resulted in the employment of more men than necessary to do a job, and that it could give
the trade unions substantial control over recruitment and dismissal. There had been great
pressure for change from the National Association of Port Employers and the scheme was
finally disbanded in 1989, with the National Dock Labour Board itself being wound up
on 30 June 1990.

In February 1978 a landmark agreement was reached in Southampton between the registered dockers and the British Transport Docks Board on the manning arrangements for
the new Container Port berth that was intended for the handling of imports and exports to
South Africa. This agreement paved the way for changes that were beneficial to all. When
the Dock Labour Scheme finally ended, Southampton Docks were owned by Associated
British Ports. Stuart Bradley, the Managing Director, made it clear that: 'Our new labour
systems do not take away trade union rights, [nor do they] replicate the dark days of nine-
teenth-century repression'. The dock management wanted to put modern arrangements in
place that gave excellent rewards to a multi-skilled workforce that was adaptable and able
to undertake a wide variety of tasks. The workforce was streamlined, and 1,000 of the 1,720
former registered dock workers took voluntary severance packages.

In Southampton, the system that evolved meant that none of the dockers were employed
by ABP. Two independent stevedoring firms emerged to handle the work, each with its
own specialisms. Southampton Cargo Handling PLC, Britain's largest worker-owned stevedoring company, was formed in April 1990 by former employees of the National Dock
Labour Scheme. It specialises in passenger and general cargo work, and deep-sea ro-ro
operations. Berkley Handling Ltd was formed in the summer of 1989 and was mainly
concerned with the vehicle trade, both being licensed by ABP to operate within the
Docks. Berkley later became part of Amports (UK) Ltd, which itself is a subsidiary of ABP.
There are other operators in the field such as Solent Stevedores Ltd and South Coast Port
Services, which specialise in mooring ships and rope running. This latter firm, which was
formed in April 1984, was founded on the earlier business of Matthews Brothers. The terminal operators also have their own direct labour forces to run these facilities.

The Shipping Federation was formed by ship owners in 1890 to promote their interests.
Initially the federation had feared the rise of organised groups of seafarers, particularly the
National Amalgamated Sailors' & Firemen's Union of Great Britain & Ireland, established

by Joseph Havelock Wilson in 1887, as they were seen as a constraint on free enterprise. The NASFU were forced to disband in 1894, but the federation mellowed its tone after the 1911 sailors' and dock workers' strike, and began to work with the unions, recognising the National Union of Seamen, of which Wilson became President in 1912. It also became involved in the training of seafarers and, after the First World War, established National Sea Training Schools in major ports. The Southampton school, which opened in the summer of 1926, was located at 19 Berth on the Eastern Docks and provided courses for the Lifeboatman's Certificate and the Efficient Deck Hands' Certificate. There were davits on the quayside on which the trainees could practice, and although the establishment closed down for the Second World War, it reopened in October 1947.

The Shipping Federation's first premises in Southampton were at 80a High Street and were acquired in 1908. In 1912 the offices moved to Canute Road. Occupation of these premises was short-lived as more room was required after the First World War, so the federation moved to what had been the Grain Office in the Eastern Docks, and remained there until the building was lost to enemy action in the Second World War. With a vital role to play during the war, the activities of the federation continued and temporary offices were established, first in Royal Mail House and then in railway premises in Terminus Terrace. These last 'temporary' offices were finally vacated on 19 January 1961 when the Shipping Federation moved to an entirely new building at 19–23 Canute Road. The opening ceremony was performed by Sir Donald Anderson, Chairman of P&O-Orient Line. Recruitment of personnel to crew the merchant fleet was a primary role of the federation, and in 1907 medical examinations were instituted. The Southampton office employed two medical officers and the facilities that were available by 1961 included an X-ray unit.

Many members of the Shipping Federation were also members of the Chamber of Shipping. These organisations merged in March 1975 to form the General Council of British Shipping, based in the same offices in Canute Road. The name of the joint body reverted to that of the Chamber of Shipping in 1991.

The *Port Handbook* of 1987-88 particularly mentions that in recent times labour relations had improved and customer confidence been regained. In fact, Southampton seems to have had very reasonable industrial relations itself and not to have been rendered entirely helpless by the actions of others. In addition to the events already mentioned, there were major strikes of both dockers and seamen in 1872 and in 1890, just after the opening of the Empress Dock. This stoppage led to the formation of a Free Labour Association, comprising both employers and employees, and seems to have gone a long way towards creating an atmosphere of mutual understanding.

There was a dock labourers' strike in 1924 and an unofficial seamen's strike in 1925, but during the coal strike and General Strike of 1926, the *Shipping Guide* wrote that these 'had little effect' on the Docks. Likewise, there was no complete stoppage during the long lay-up of the 1966 seamen's strike. There was also a five-week strike by maintenance staff in April-May 1978.

The press seems to have been almost entirely complimentary to the dock workers in Southampton. In 1978 the owner of ABC Line, at the start of a new container service to Australia, was quoted as saying, 'Here is a vessel that the men are totally unfamiliar with, yet they are working her as if they had been doing it for years. I never expected anything like this'. As another example, Mann & Sons praised the dock workers for 'loading cars in appalling weather' in January 1984.

5

# THE FUNCTIONING PORT

## BUNKERING

Ships calling at Southampton very often require fuel before continuing their journeys. In the early days of steam power this was exclusively coal, which was delivered in barges alongside the ships and laboriously hoisted on-board in baskets, a process known locally as 'dollying'. It was a slow business and the bunkering record of 4,000 tons loaded on the *Olympic* in August 1912 took eighteen hours. It seems odd given the long history of the port that the coal barge dock, which could store 20,000 tons of coal afloat in barges, was not created until October 1903. There was also some mechanical assistance in the form of a floating coal hoist from about 1910. This was sunk at 22 Berth in an air raid of November 1940.

R. & J.H. Rea came to Southampton in 1893 and gained contracts to supply Royal Mail in 1895, Union Castle in 1900 and White Star in 1910, becoming the principal suppliers of bunker coal. Rea took over the Southampton business of its competitor, the Powell Duffryn Steam Coal Co. in 1914, and itself became part of W.M. Cory & Son Ltd in 1918. During the First World War, the advantages of burning oil to raise steam were recognised and many steamships began to use oil instead of coal as a fuel. The first ship to sail from Southampton burning oil was the *Olympic* after conversion in June 1920. Her fuel was supplied by the British-Mexican Petroleum Co. Ltd which started operating in Southampton using tank barges, but also had land-based storage of 52,000 tons by 1923.

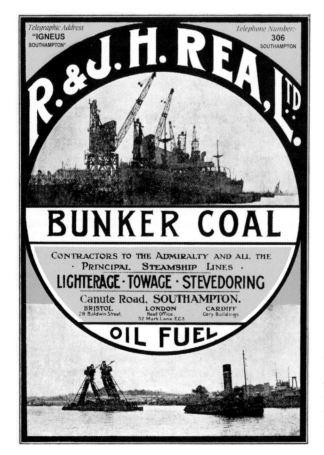

Advertisement from the early 1920s for R. & J.H. Rea Ltd, suppliers of bunker coal. By this time there was a barge-mounted mechanical elevator, shown here, to assist in the coaling of ships. (Private collection)

Agwi Petroleum Corporation Ltd with its refinery close by had land-based storage for bunkering of 99,000 tons in 1923, rising to 211,000 tons in 1933 and 253,000 tons in 1936. The Anglo American Oil Co. had two depot ships for storage and supply of bunker oil, *Genesee* and *Silvertown*, which were moored in Southampton Water in the early 1920s, but these were replaced by land storage facilities in 1924. Shell-Mex Ltd also had the tanker *Prygona* on hand, although she was replaced by land storage tanks in 1925. Rea were local agents for the Anglo-Persian Oil Co. from 1922 and used the tanker *Britsh Maple*. By the time these firms were joined by the independent supplier Hemsley Bell Ltd in 1925, Southampton had become one of the principal ports in the UK for supplying fuel oil to ships. Such was the rise in the popularity of oil that over 400,000 tons were supplied for ships' bunkers in 1933, and by 1951 the majority of ships were oil fuelled. There were then three principal suppliers in Southampton: British-Mexican Petroleum Co. Ltd at Woolston; Esso at Fawley; and Shell Mex and BP on the Hamble. John H. Whittaker (Tankers) Ltd have supplied Esso bunker fuels in Southampton since 1988.

The *Hampshire Independent* noted when Inner Dock was opened in 1851 that it was for colliers bringing coal mainly from the north-east of England and for sailing ships of all kinds. Some of the coal brought in was for distribution in the hinterland rather than for bunkering, and a device was constructed at 13 Berth in 1865 for unloading colliers. It was used first by the Hill firm and later by J.R. Wood & Co. In the 1890s the coal depot was leased to the Southampton Steamship Coal & Patent Fuel Co. After unloading, the coal was graded into different sizes and the finest material was converted into briquettes for household use, which were said to be very popular in the town.

## POLICE

In 1838 the Corporation Watch Committee first employed a policeman for the protection of passengers at the pier and quay, although this facility was paid for by the Harbour Commissioners. The foundation of a separate body to look after the interests of the Docks soon followed. Two watchmen were employed to protect the works during construction and from 1839 they wore police uniform. This force grew so that even before the opening of Itchen Quay it comprised an inspector, two sergeants and eight permanent constables. The Dock Police had experienced trying moments where assistance was required, most notably in March 1854 when the town police were called in to assist in order to control the crowds that had amassed to see the departure of the *Ripon* and *Manilla* for the Crimea. The departure of troop ships caused regular displays of patriotic fervour until the outbreak of the First World War and the exclusion of the public from the quays.

When the London & South Western Railway took control in 1892 the Dock Police, which by now had expanded to one inspector, three sergeants, eleven uniformed constables and two plain-clothes constables, was absorbed into the railway's own security system. Their jurisdiction then extended to include all railway lines and premises of the LSWR and, later, those of the Southern Railway. On the nationalisation of the railways in 1948, all railway police became part of the British Transport Commission Police. A Divisional Superintendent was now in charge of the local area. Moving with the times, the division then developed a detective department and, in 1953, employed its first policewoman. During 1963, four police dogs were added specifically to work in the Docks and

The Dock Police Station in Central Road, just behind the Dock Post Office, as it appeared in the 1920s. The single-storey Police Annexe was constructed on the other side of the road in 1952, with a first floor being added in 1960. (Author)

at the end of that year the boundaries of the Southampton Division were redefined so that it encompassed only the Docks, while policing of the main railway lines was supervised from Waterloo. The original Police Office was behind the Dock Post Office. A single-storey Police Annexe was built in 1952, also in Central Road, and this had a first floor added in 1960.

Since the privatisation of the Docks security arrangements have been subcontracted, although Hampshire Constabulary had a Water Section that operated the launch *Versatile* from Southampton. When *Versatile* was replaced by *Ashburton* in 1971, the new Marine Subdivision moved to the Isle of Wight.

## CUSTOMS

Customs officers were appointed at major ports in 1298 to collect the King's 'customary dues', although the Board of Customs was not formed until 1643. The first purpose-built Customs House in Southampton was opened in 1733 on the site of the Corn Exchange, opposite Town Quay. This building was demolished when the office was transferred to a new building in 1847 and is now known as Union Castle House. The Customs Service did not, however, own the building outright and when the lease came up for renewal in 1892 they moved again to the former P&O offices in Canute Road. A new Customs building, designed by Hawke, was erected in 1902 on the site of the Dock Carpenters' Shop and adjacent to the 1847 building.

The customs and excise functions of the government were amalgamated in 1909 to form HM Customs & Excise. This body continued to use the 1902 headquarters until an imposing ten-storey glass and concrete building to the design of the Ministry of Public Buildings & Works was erected on the corner of Briton Street and Orchard Place, with its entrance facing Queen's Park. When opened on 7 March 1966 by Sir Wilfred Morton, Chairman of the Board of Customs & Excise, it was the tallest building in the dockland area and has only recently been demolished. A new four-storey concrete building was erected on the site of the 1902 offices by Dock Gate 4. Named Portcullis House, it was opened on 6 June 1973 by Sir Louis Petch, successor to Sir Wilfred Morton. It was intended to house the Waterguard, which was formed in 1923 and had been located in various buildings round the Docks. This body of uniformed officers collected dues from the passengers and crew of ships and also had a role in deterring smuggling. In 1972 Customs & Excise was restructured and the Waterguard was fully integrated with Customs staff. Also in January 1973, Britain joined the EEC and there were further changes to the function of Customs and Excise, which was amalgamated with the Inland Revenue to form HM Revenue & Customs in 2005. The most recent development, in 2009, is that the preventive functions formerly carried out by the Waterguard have been transferred to the UK Border Agency of the Home Office.

The smooth flow of goods relies on proper documentation, the ever increasing volume of which proved to be a problem to Customs. A new system to ease freight processing was pioneered in Southampton in the autumn of 1985. Called Direct Trader Input or DTI, this is a computer system which allows users to submit details electronically directly to the Customs network.

The building known today as Union Castle House was designed by Giles and built in 1857, becoming the offices of Union Line in 1892. It is shown as it appeared in about 1930, the projecting stone frontage having been added early in the twentieth century. (Author)

The Customs building on Canute Road, built in 1902 and quite new when this photograph was taken. The present Dock Gate 4 is located on the right by the iron railings. This building was replaced by the flat-roofed Portcullis House in 1973. (Brain collection)

Up to 1869, Customs had a revenue cutter called *Harpy* moored at Itchen Spit to report the arrival of ships. With the advent of the electric telegraph, Customs no longer needed her, but she had become a useful navigational aid and was bought by the Harbour Board and converted into a lightship, a duty she performed until the growth of the Docks rendered her purpose unnecessary. Preventive officers patrolled Southampton Water in Revenue launches and had their own boat house at 4 Berth. From the Second World War to the 1970s, these vessels were successively *Vigilant*, *Venturous* and *Valiant*.

Locally the Collector, based in the Custom House, was responsible for functions that we would now associate with other agencies. He was the Registrar of British Ships, Receiver of Wrecks and Collector of Light Dues.

## IMMIGRATION SERVICE

One of the few people allowed on-board a ship on entering the port from foreign waters, apart from the pilot and Customs Officer, was an officer from the Immigration Service, a branch of the Home Office. In Southampton there were forty-four of these non-uniformed personnel, together with five Chief Immigration Officers and a District Inspector. They controlled foreign and Commonwealth seamen as well as passengers coming from abroad, initially under the Aliens Act of 1905. The original offices were in Havelock Chambers, Queen's Terrace.

In 1971, the Immigration Service moved from offices it occupied at 149a High Street to the premises of the former Parsons Engineering Co. at Town Quay, and at almost the same time appointed its first two female staff. Vessels coming into Southampton are no longer met in this way, but e-Borders, the UK Border Agency's electronic border control system, allows the checking of passenger and crew before they enter or leave the UK.

## ARRIVAL OF THE MARITIME & COASTGUARD AGENCY

The growth of yachting and pleasure boat sailing in the area prompted HM Coastguard to create a search and rescue station at Calshot, which opened in November 1970. In 1998 the activities of HM Coastguard and the Maritime Safety Agency were combined and its headquarters established in Southampton, with a number of Coastguard and Survey offices around the country. As a government agency, it is responsible for UK maritime policy and the coastguard system. The MCA's responsibilities range from ship registration and regulation to protecting the marine environment, from saving life at sea to representing UK maritime interests at international forums, such as the International Maritime Organisation, at which international standards for shipping are developed.

## PILOTS

No doubt guidance to mariners has been required for centuries, but it was only in 1808 that the Isle of Wight Pilotage District was formed by the Corporation of Trinity House, and pilots were not specifically licensed to conduct vessels to and from Southampton until 1842. There was keen competition, with pilots owning their own sailing cutters and

The Maritime & Coastguard Agency headquarters at Spring Place, 105 Commercial Road, Southampton. Lloyd's Register of Shipping is also now housed here. (Author)

vying with each other to be the first to reach a vessel in order to claim the payment for bringing the ship safely in to port. In 1822 there were thirty-eight pilot cutters operating in the Isle of Wight District, often, like the Bowyers in Southampton, with several generations of the same family succeeding each other as licensed pilots.

Towards the end of the nineteenth century, manned sea cutters were moored at fixed places, such as at the extremities of the Isle of Wight, the Nab and the Needles, and off Netley Abbey. Launches would take pilots to and from these points as required for the guidance of shipping. The service was further subdivided into inward pilots and outward pilots. The inward pilots brought a vessel from sea to Netley, from which point the outward pilot, as well as having other responsibilities, would take the vessel into Southampton (and back again in due time – hence the 'outward' part of the title). The old Netley cutter was withdrawn at the end of the Second World War and the actual base for pilots became the Naval Pier at Hythe. As noted elsewhere, the Port Communications Centre at 37 Berth became active in July 1972 and thereafter became the base for pilots and also for the six Trinity House Sub-Commissioners, the persons responsible for the selection and licensing of pilots. The boarding point for pilots later became Gosport. From 1 October 1988, the provision of qualified pilots was no longer under the control of Trinity House but became the responsibility of the competent Harbour Authority in any particular place. In Southampton that was and is Associated British Ports. It should be pointed out that the use of a pilot is compulsory for merchant ships, with few exceptions.

The pilotage launches themselves are based in Southampton. Mention must be made of the *Protector*, which was launched in 1993 as the harbour patrol launch, primarily for the Harbour Master to examine the port infrastructure and see that bylaws were being obeyed, but she could also act as a reserve pilot boat. Subsequent vessels, *Portunus* and *Prospect* have continued this dual role. Another launch of the pilotage service was *Jessica* which, when she came into service in early 1957, was the first pilot boat in Britain to have a glass-reinforced plastic hull.

## PORT HEALTH AND QUARANTINE

Southampton has been described as one of the entry points for plague into England, particularly by the Augustinian canon Henry Knighton, who was writing in the latter part of the fourteenth century. Although his view that 'the grievous plague came to the sea coasts from Southampton' has since been disputed, it remains true that communicable diseases can easily be brought to a port and that continued vigilance is necessary.

The likelihood of outbreaks of serious communicable diseases brought from abroad was high. Southampton became the headquarters of Hamburg America Line for a period in 1892 when an outbreak of cholera forced the company to leave its home port. Southampton Borough Council became the Port Health Authority in 1893 as a result of regulations made by the Local Government Board. One of the first actions of the new authority was the purchase of the redundant clipper and former emigrant ship *City of Adelaide* for use as a floating isolation hospital.

Today there are other means of control such as inoculation, and smallpox has been eradicated. *City of Adelaide* was sold in 1923, but non-military cases of acute infectious disease coming by sea were removed to Southampton Isolation Hospital and cases of smallpox to the huts at Millbrook Marsh. The Port Health Authority, which had its seaward boundaries extended in 1935, had a launch with which to visit and inspect suspect vessels and in 1926 recorded that the number of cases of infectious disease occurring on ships was 1,162.

Diseases requiring quarantine and the method of handling them have, since the Second World War, been regulated by the World Health Organisation. The Environmental Health Department of Southampton City Council continues to be responsible for port health and, following the Borough Council role, supervises the living conditions of crew on-board merchant ships and inspects imported foodstuffs to see that they are fit for human consumption. The control of pests such as rodents is also part of this regime.

The precautions taken by the city to safeguard the health of passengers and crew were noticed by the shipping companies, and in the early 1920s the United States Line, Royal Mail and White Star all used 'Bono', the super vermicide from the Steamship Specialities Supply Co. in the High Street. The ships painters and decorators, John Wright & Son, also offered a fumigation service.

Today we associate quarantine with animals. Southampton has, almost from the creation of the Docks, been a centre for the importation of cattle and even exotic animals. In the 1950s it was the only port licensed by the government for the import of Jersey cattle, which were often re-exported. The only other British Transport Docks Board ports designated for the import of animals was Hull, in the north-east of England. Unlike Southampton, Hull did not have the short-term holding facilities introduced in Southampton in 1976, when a new purpose-built and state-of-the-art quarantine centre was built in the Docks by J.S.L. Ltd in 1983.

## EMERGENCY RESPONSE

The LSWR had a fireboat stationed in the Docks, but it was the SR that created a land-based fire station in 1923 staffed by a Superintendent, a Leading Fireman and seven permanent firefighters, supplemented by ten auxiliaries. The last job of the Dock Fire Brigade was to tackle the blaze at the International Cold Store following an air raid in 1940, for which it required the assistance of other brigades. Shortly after that, the National Fire Service was created. After the Second World War, responsibility for tackling fire lay with Southampton Fire Brigade, which took over the NFS fire boats in the Docks. The Southampton brigade was innovative in creating a special jet pump in 1954 to minimise the listing of ships when sprayed with water, and eight of these were subsequently built. The last fireboat was delivered by Thornycroft in 1963. It passed to Hampshire Fire Brigade and was sold in 1987.

Prompted by the possibility of a collision, oil spill or related incident, particularly involving tankers in such a busy waterway, British Transport Docks Board established an emergency plan in 1970 to deal with any incidents; it was known as the Solent and Southampton Water Marine Emergency Plan, or 'Solfire'. This voluntary scheme involves Naval Command in Portsmouth, police, fire brigades, medical services, hospitals and organisations dealing with oil pollution, rescue and welfare. It has regular exercises and is updated and broadened in scope as necessary. 'Solspill', the oil spill contingency plan, was added in 1993. There have been other such emergency responses in the past, for example the Air Raid Precautions night exercise of 15-16 July 1937, when the entire harbour area was blacked out. Today Southampton follows the UK Port Marine Safety Code and the harbour patrol launches and hydrographic survey form part of this process.

BP established an oil spill response facility to meet its own needs in 1980, and in 1984 Oil Spill Response Ltd was formed in order to offer its services to others. It is now the largest and most advanced response unit in the world and operates locally from a jetty on the River Itchen.

Particularly with the demise of fire floats, tugs have been equipped for fire-fighting. The Red Funnel tugs *Gatcombe* and *Vecta* were stationed at Fawley marine terminal in 1971 for this purpose. Subsequently Solent Towage Ltd, a subsidiary of Johannes ØstensjØdij of Norway, was in 1995, awarded the contract by Esso Petroleum Ltd for berthing, fire-fighting, escort and anti-pollution services at Fawley Marine Terminal.


## RESEARCH

Surveying and patrolling the Antarctic began as a Naval exercise, codenamed 'Operation Tabarin', towards the end of 1943. After the Second World War this became the Falklands Islands Dependencies Survey.

Occupied bases in the Antarctic were originally relieved by chartered vessels, but in 1947 the former net-layer HMS *Pretext* was acquired, converted and renamed *John Biscoe*. Another ship, *Norsel*, was chartered at the end of 1954. A Swedish cargo ship *Arendal* was acquired, renamed *Shackleton*, and put into service in 1955. A new *John Biscoe*, specially built for working in ice, was constructed in Paisley and launched in June 1956, making her maiden voyage from Southampton on 26 November. The original *John Biscoe* was sold to the New Zealand government.

All these craft were granted the title of Royal Research Ships by the Queen. Their duty was to take supplies and relieve the personnel who were engaged in exploration and scientific research at bases in the British sector of Antarctica. The tour of duty for each vessel was up to eight months, during which time they had to sail through some of the most challenging and dangerous waters on Earth.

In October 1959, the Danish ship *Kista Dan* was chartered for survey work and remained on charter until 1966. The name of the operation was changed to the

'British Antarctic Survey' in February 1962. British Antarctic Survey also chartered the *Perla Dan* from Lauritzen Line, which sailed on her first mission in November 1968. The RRS *Shackleton* was retired on her return from duty in 1970 and replaced by another new vessel, RRS *Bransfield*, then the most advanced polar research ship in the world. *Bransfield's* first tour of duty began on the 4 January 1971 and took her further south than any ship had ever been. The research ships were maintained by J.I. Thornycroft and could often be seen in the Outer Dock. They were even more visible from October 1960, when *John Biscoe* was painted bright red. *John Biscoe* was modernised in 1980 and in the mid-1980s both research ships moved to a new base in Grimsby.

It was announced in March 1989 that a £35 million ocean study centre was to be built on a 13 acre (5.3 hectare) site at 26 and 27 Berths in Empress Dock. This government-funded project was a joint initiative of the Natural Environmental Research Council and the University of Southampton, a Select Committee of the House of Lords having recommended such a collaborative effort in December 1985. The building contract was awarded to Wimpey Construction Ltd and work started in the spring of 1993. Now known as the National Oceanography Centre, it was opened by Prince Philip in March 1996 and, as a result, Royal Research Ships *Discovery* and *Charles Darwin* returned to Southampton. *Charles Darwin* was retired in 2006 and replaced by *James Cook*, making her maiden voyage in March 2007. The university also has its own research vessel, *Callista*.

In 1993 ABP Research & Consultancy Ltd moved to a purpose-built research centre at Pathfinder House, near Ocean Village, in a new building designed and constructed by the Southampton-based Brazier Group.

The unit had originally been set up in 1950 by the Docks and Inland Waterways Executive and operated from premises in Southall, Middlesex. In 1963 this came under the control of the British Transport Docks Board in order to provide for the needs of the nationalised dock industry. From 1983 it was known as ABP Research & Consultancy Ltd, concentrating on hydraulic modelling, operational research and hydrographic surveying.

A hydrographic survey launch, *Trumpeter*, was based in Southampton Docks from the early 1950s. She was fitted with a Kelvin Hughes recording echo sounder that enabled quick and accurate estimates to be made of the rate of silting and subsequent need for dredging of channels and berths. Although fitted with a new superstructure, the hull was a product of the British Power Boat Co. of Hythe.

In 2002 the research facility was renamed ABP Marine Environmental Research Ltd to reflect its increasingly diverse work, for it offers solutions to coastal, estuary, river and inland-waterway environmental and development problems, both to ABP and on a commercial basis to anyone else who wishes to use its facilities. The facility later moved to Waterside House, Town Quay.

## EVENTS

The locally based and recently formed Motor Yacht Club was asked to organise the races for motorboats for the 1908 London Olympic Games. The three races that made up the event were to take place in Southampton Water on 28-29 August, a month after the sailing events which were held off Ryde. Along with tug-of-war, this was the first and last appearance of this sport at an Olympiad.

The weather during the whole of the games had not been good and conditions were very bad for the motorboat races. The water was choppy, there was a gale blowing and a report of the competition later noted, 'That any competitors started at all was a strong testimony to their pluck and determination'.

In Class A, open to all comers, there were three participants: the Duke of Westminster with *Wolseley-Siddeley*, Lord Howard de Walden with *Dylan*, and a French contestant Emile Thubron with *Camille*. Thubron was the only contestant to finish the forty-mile course and therefore won the gold medal. The Class B race was for vessels under 60ft (18.3m) in length, and the Class C was for those between 6.5 and 8 metres. I.T. Thornycroft, who had designed his own beetle-shaped *Gyrinus II* and had it built by the family firm, participated in both races. He had only one opponent in each race, John Marshall Gorham in *Quicksilver* and Warwick Wright in *Sea Dog* respectively, and as neither of these completed the course, 'Tom' Thornycroft became a double gold medallist.

Merchant Navy Week was a unique event held in the Docks in the sheds and waterfront at 107 and 108 Berths from 17-24 July 1937, and was designed as a fundraising event for the Missions to Seamen. There were eight main sections. The first was about the equipment used by the seafarer, and the remaining seven were designed to show ordinary citizens the impact that the work of the seafarer had on them by making significant contributions to their housing, warmth, food, clothes, leisure pursuits and how they were protected.

Other topics were covered too, including the training of seafarers and the history of navigation, and there was said to be a complete collection of the house flags of British shipping companies. Communications was covered by the General Post Office, which had what was termed a 'remarkable exhibition' showing its relationship to the Merchant Navy. The exhibition was supported by pictures, models and historical items loaned by Lloyds, such as relics from the *Lutine* and the *Drummond Castle*, and there were numerous demonstrations. The show was enlivened by drill performances and dancing by boys from training ships and nautical schools, and there were film shows and deck games with floodlighting and fireworks in the evenings to add to the atmosphere. Ships nearby were open to the public, including the battleship HMS *Revenge* and the new cruiser HMS *Southampton*. Posters advertising the event were drawn by well-known marine artist Kenneth Shoesmith, which no doubt contributed to the numbers of visitors who were brought to the show on special rail excursions laid on by the Dock owners.

A peculiarity of the event was a daily opening ceremony. The first, or perhaps the official, opening was by Princess Alice, the Countess of Athlone, whose husband was the President of the Exhibition, but the opening of the show on the 20th, for example, was by the Lord Mayor of London. How this was received in Southampton is not recorded.

The Festival of Britain in 1951 was a national event especially designed to add a little gaiety to peoples' lives after the stresses and privations of wartime. The Dock Co. also hoped for an increase in passenger traffic owing to the numbers of people coming to visit it. The main events were in London, at which the Shipping Section on the South Bank displayed the Southampton Dock Model created for the 1939 New York World's Fair, as well as a separate model of the new Ocean Terminal, but there were regional activities too. Southampton's contribution to the event was a Shipping and Industries Exhibition in Blighmont Drill Hall, which was opened on 30 June 1951 by Earl Mountbatten of Burma. The Festival of Britain ship *Campania* came to the New Docks and was open to the public from the 4-14 May. Southampton was the first of ten ports of call and she attracted 80,000 people from the immediate area. There was also a Festival of Britain stand erected in the first-class reception hall of Ocean Terminal for the benefit of newly arrived visitors to the UK. Before the end of the festival in September, the destroyers HMS *Solebay* and HMS *St Kitts* visited the New Docks as part of the celebrations and attracted over 3,000 visitors.

There had been a boating section at the Southampton Show of 1963 which gained some interest, and subsequently the Council had discussed the potential for developing this theme with the Hampshire Boat Builders' Federation. Things progressed as far as a search for a potential site, but that initiative was not developed. The Southampton Boat Show in its present form, the creation of two local businessmen, started in September 1969, sixteen years after the London Boat Show based in Olympia. While initially very small in comparison, it has had one great advantage from the outset – that craft can be exhibited in their natural environment on the water. The original pontoon, a small 'T'-shaped structure, came from Marchwood and was loaned by the Army. By 1971, there were two pontoons displaying fifty boats. The number had grown to 100 by 1973 and 254 by 1988. In 2008, the grid of pontoons extended over an area larger than Mayflower Park itself and there were over 300 floating exhibits.

The first Boat Show in Southampton was opened by Alderman Kathy Johnson and ran for six days. By 1973, there were 55,000 visitors and the numbers increased to 70,000 in 1974, 90,000 in 1977, and 125,000 in 1989, the show's twenty-first-year, when it was also described as 'Europe's biggest'. The following year the show was billed as Southampton International Boat Show and it continues to draw exhibitors and visitors from around the world. The original organisers handed over to the Ship & Boat Builders' National Federation in 1981, and it has continued to grow both in size and in duration. It first spread inland, crossing Herbert Walker Avenue to the triangle of land in front of Post House Hotel (now the Holiday Inn) and had completely enveloped the hotel by 1977. In the early 1980s it crossed West Quay Road to occupy the site of the present Grand Harbour Hotel, moving slightly further west when this site was developed. In the twenty-first century it has both spread further north across Western Esplanade and from 2006 has temporarily taken over 101 Berth in the Western Docks. The show reached its present length of ten days in 1997.

The nucleus of the event has, from its very beginning, been at Mayflower Park. The naming of the park, after the ship in which the Pilgrim Fathers sailed to America, is a post-war development almost coinciding with the creation of the Boat Show. The park was created at the time the New or, as they later became known, Western Docks were built and had previously been known as the Corporation Recreation Ground or the Royal Pier Recreation Ground.

The original location of the Boat Show was, in the 1950s, also the site of the Town Regatta, with 101 Berth also being made accessible in 1957 for the visit of HMS *Grafton*, which was open to the public. There had been a Town Regatta, usually held in September, since the 1840s, although the event is now held towards the end of May.

## RELIGIOUS EVENTS AND WELFARE FACILITIES

A feature of the beginning of the modern commercial Docks was the religious service held in All Saints Church. Early in the history of the Dock Co., an appeal was received from Revd Dr Wilson of Holy Rood for financial assistance for the repairing of the Chapel of God's House. The company gave £50, a not inconsiderable sum at the time, which was stated to be out of 'religious obligation' and for the 'peace and welfare of the town'. The

The Boat Show on Mayflower Park in about 1970. Note the road sign indicating access to Berths 101–202. Before the bridge accessing Dock Gate 20 was built, entrance to the Container Port was via this route. (Bitterne Local History Society)

Dock Co. again contributed £20 towards the building of St James' Church in Bernard Street, no doubt because the Docks were within the new parish. The land on which it was built was given by Queen's College, Oxford, and the building was consecrated on 4 October 1858.

Saint Mary's Church, regarded as the 'mother church' of Southampton, has been rebuilt several times. It was reconstructed most recently in 1956 in a traditional style, after suffering considerable damage during the Second World War. The north transept was set aside as a seamen's chapel and was dedicated by Rt Revd Leslie Lang, the assistant Bishop of Winchester, on Sunday 24 June. A stained-glass window for the chapel was designed by Gerald E.R. Smith and executed by Nicholson Studios in London, and this was unveiled by Sir William Currie, Chairman and Managing Director of P&O, at a dedication service on 27 October 1959. All the furniture was made by dockland craftsmen and the prayer desk embodies symbols essential for safe navigation: the log, lead and lookout. British Railways contributed, among other items, the bell from its steamer *Hantonia*. The intention was that this should be rung ceremonially on any occasion requiring the summoning of the people to pray for any cause concerning life at sea – danger, victory or thanksgiving. Other decoration comprised the flags of British shipping companies on the walls and ship models that have lately been removed. Another bell, which came from the Calshot Spit light vessel, was presented for safekeeping by the Elder Brethren of Trinity House in September 1972, as it was no longer needed for sounding watches on an unmanned ship. For the first twenty or so years of its existence, the seamen's chapel held regular prayers for the 'ship of the week'. The chosen vessel had its photograph and details exhibited as well as its position at the time. Many vessels were included; some of the first were *Arcadia*,

*Mauretania*, *New Australia*, *Pretoria Castle* and *Southern Cross*. The practice was abandoned in the 1980s.

The annual Shipping Festival was instigated by Southampton Master Mariners' Club, the 'Cachalots', in 1928 and was originally held in All Saints Church in Southampton. In 1931 the venue was moved to Holy Rood Church and the following year moved again, to Winchester Cathedral. After an interval during the Second World War, it was revived on 12 July 1950 and continues in the cathedral to this day, except that the service is normally in mid-June. There are sermons relevant to current maritime events and in 1969 the Master Mariners presented the Red Ensign from the *Queen Elizabeth* to the cathedral.

Both Holy Rood and All Saints Churches were lost during the Second World War, but the shell of Holy Rood was dedicated as a Merchant Navy Memorial. A plaque was unveiled by the Bishop of Southampton on 17 April 1957 which reads: 'Known for centuries as the Church of the Sailors, the ruins have been preserved by the people of Southampton as a memorial and Garden of rest to those who served in the Merchant Navy and lost their lives at sea'. Its position has been consolidated by the incorporation of other tributes. A monument, in the form of a drinking fountain, to stewards, sailors and firemen who lost their lives in the *Titanic* disaster was moved there from a site on Southampton Common and was re-dedicated on 15 April 1972 at a civic service by the Mayor's Chaplain, the Revd R.J. Milner. A wreath was laid by the Mayor of Southampton, Alderman J. Barr, and one on behalf of the British Transport Docks Board, Southampton, was laid by the Dock and Harbour Master, Captain E.J. Kirton. More recently a plaque was erected by the City Council to mark the '... invaluable and heroic service of the Merchant Navy operating out of the Port of Southampton in the campaign to recover the Falkland Islands...'. As befits such an important edifice, the site continues to be cared for and improved by the city.

The annual Port of Southampton New Year service in the Seamen's Chapel at Southampton Seafarers' Centre (formerly the Missions to Seamen), which is the only one of its kind in any British port, is another tradition that continues to the present day, although of relatively recent foundation. It started in about 1936, and seems to have been displaced only once from the first working day of the New Year. That was in 1969, when the new *Queen Elizabeth 2* was scheduled to arrive at 9.30 a.m. on Wednesday 1 January and it was feared that the congregation would be greatly depleted.

In May 1950 the vicar of the then Dockland Parish Church of St James, in cooperation with other clerics, started the observance of Rogation Sunday with a service at Town Quay and at the Old Docks, in order to bless the waters and shipping. This continued annually until about 1960 with varying degrees of ceremony. The officiating priest in the early years took to the water on-board the fifty-year-old Missions to Seamen's launch *Mendell* and from 1952 used her replacement, *Princess Elizabeth*. Although short-lived, this ceremony was the equivalent of the more familiar 'beating the bounds', or parading round the outer boundaries of a parish. This ceremony has been continued in Southampton for centuries on a date just prior to the Court Leet, which takes place in late September or early October. Today only a token re-establishing of the boundaries is undertaken and is usually confined to the land, but on 15 September 1951, the 500th anniversary of the creation of the office of Admiral of the Port, the Mayor, as Admiral, sailed round the Docks in the motor vessel *Balmoral*, with ships in port being dressed overall for the occasion and saluting with their sirens.

There are other unique and equally poignant memorials in the city that relate directly to the Docks. In Hollybrook Cemetery, a substantial section is maintained by the War Graves Commission. It is on a slight slope and, with white Portland stone in an arc and with an inverted sword at the centre it is, in outward appearance, like many others throughout the world. This, however, is like no other. It is '… in memory of the 1,852 officers and men of the British Empire who fell in the Great War and who have no known grave but the sea…'. It begins with the name of the Secretary of State for War, Field Marshal Kitchener of Khartoum, who was lost on HMS *Hampshire*, but also includes members of the Royal Naval Reserve, the Merchant Marine and quite a few members of Queen Alexandra's Imperial Military Nursing Service. As many of the vessels on which these people served were troop transports or hospital ships, they have a direct connection with Southampton, which was the principal military port at the time.

Outside the old Dock Offices, now called Ferry House, are two almost identical memorials to the railway servants who lost their lives, one during the First World War with seventy-five names, and one during the Second World War with forty-three names.

The welfare of today's seafarers is coordinated by Southampton Port Welfare Committee, which is made up of representatives from ship owners, officers and sea-farers' associations, and voluntary and other organizations. The committee itself forms an advisory group to the Merchant Navy Welfare Board. The Merchant Navy Welfare Board at one time used to include a representative from the Ministry of Transport and to receive an element of government funding via a levy on British ship owners employing non-domiciled seamen, but this was withdrawn in the early 1970s. The Merchant Navy Welfare Board itself was established in London in 1948, although its predecessor as coordinating body had been established in 1927.

The British Sailors' Society was the first of the voluntary welfare organisations to be established in the port in 1837. The society had been founded by a group of businessmen who wished to alleviate the conditions then endured by merchant seamen. This was followed in Southampton by the Missions to Seamen in 1856, although the actual South Coast Ports area headquarters was in Ryde on the Isle of Wight.

The need for a residence for seafarers in Southampton seems to have been recorded first in 1841 in a book entitled *Southampton and its Commercial Prospects* where, in the chapter on the domestication of sailors and the labouring classes, the following is recorded:

> … [for] the sailor, however, a different provision is required. He is generally without a home, his stay in port is temporary, and he too often becomes the prey of the crafty and the vicious. Every commercial port should be provided with sailors' barracks, where they might find the asylum they require. These barracks might be of a twofold character, on shore and afloat. The latter in many respects, the more desirable…

The independent Southampton Sailors' Home opened in 1861 with premises on the north side of Canute Road before it moved to a new building in Oxford Street in 1909. It closed its doors sixty years later when the building was sold to the Salvation Army. Other residential facilities were provided by Toc H through Talbot House, it's Seafaring Boys' Residential Club. In the slump of the 1920s, Revd L.G. Meade, the local head, determined that something practical had to be done for young sea-

The former Sailors' Home in Oxford Street photographed in the ownership of the Salvation Army. The third floor was skilfully added in 1912, preserving the integrity of the façade. (Author)

farers who were idle and penniless. An empty shop in Orchard Lane was acquired and adapted to form a makeshift hostel in 1924 and this functioned until the first purpose-built hostel was opened at the corner of Bernard Street and Brunswick Square in 1932. This building was remodelled, extended and reopened on 10 April 1959 by Admiral Sir William Tennant, Chairman of King George's Fund for Sailors, which was the major funding body. The final move was to a new building, also called Talbot House, in Queensway in around 1970. By this time its primary function was to act as a residence for engineer cadets attending Southampton College of Technology and, as a review of 1974 stated, if it had not been for them, 'Talbot House would have had to close its doors years ago'. Pay and conditions on-board ship had improved considerably, there were fewer young deckhands needed and they no longer had to hang about hoping to be signed on.

Further accommodation was provided for seafarers in the Jellicoe Memorial Sailors' Hostel in Orchard Place facing Queen's Park, the foundation stone of which was laid by Lady Jellicoe in February 1936. This was owned and operated by what was then known as the British Sailors' Society, whose Port Missionary had his office next door. Other facilities were provided for seafarers, such as the Ocean Library Service which was provided for the benefit of sailors on two-thirds of British ships at one time.

The six-storey Merchant Navy Hotel in Lodge Road was opened by the Merchant Navy Welfare Board on 8 May 1963, in a ceremony performed by Sir Richard Snedden, a former director of the Shipping Federation. With fifteen double rooms and thirty-eight

The Missions to Seamen as it appeared in about 1950, although it has not changed radically since it was built in 1936. The Southampton branch of the World Ship Society was formed here in 1950. (Author)

single rooms, it was designed to accommodate not only seafarers but their families too. The ground floor provided telephones, restaurant, bar, a residents' lounge and writing room, a television lounge and recreation room with the facility to unite the reception area and a restaurant for functions. At the time it was the seventh such establishment run by the board. The last of these hotels to close was the London one, in 2002, but the Merchant Navy Welfare Board then relocated its headquarters to Southampton in January 2003.

The Apostleship of the Sea was founded in Glasgow in 1922 and had a chaplain in Southampton from the 1930s, but opened the Stella Maris Club for seafarers only on 24 May 1974. This was in St Michael's Square off Bugle Street, in a building formerly occupied by St Joseph's School and comprised a bar, snack bar, television lounge, shop, telephone and postal facilities on the ground floor. A dance floor and games area were provided on the first floor above.

The first chaplain of the Missions to Seamen actually to be based in Southampton was appointed in 1868 and his 'parish' at the time included the French port of Le Havre. The foundation stone for the Chapel and Institute in Royal Crescent was laid by Prince Alfred, Duke of Edinburgh, in 1890. This remained the local headquarters until the present building in Queen's Terrace was opened by the Princess Alice, Countess of Athlone, in 1937, the Chapel of St Andrew being dedicated by the Bishop of Winchester. To mark the centenary of the Southampton 'Station', the cloister and garden of remembrance was added in 1956. Other centenary projects were to provide a television room in the institute and to present a Bible to every boy making his first trip to sea during the centenary year. Mrs Sorrell, the wife of Captain D.W. Sorrell, former Master of the *Queen Mary*, officially opened the television room on 6 March 1957, and the Bishop of Winchester dedicated the cloister and garden on 10 April. The building was refurbished and altered during 1974 so that activities were concentrated on the ground floor, and it was renamed the Flying Angel Club.

The Society for the Promotion of Christian Knowledge also had a Port Chaplain as part of its work in ministering to travellers afloat through the Church on the High Seas, but this function was transferred to the Missions to Seamen in 1966.

As early as 1973, the Missions to Seamen had identified a need for a facility for the crews of vessels using the Container Port which was far from the existing centres, and wished to do something jointly with the British Sailors' Society and the Apostleship of the Sea. In fact this never came to fruition, but these bodies, which in the interim had become respectively the Mission to Seafarers, the Sailors' Society and the Apostleship of the Sea, now operate as one from the former Flying Angel Club, under the title of the Southampton Seafarers' Centre. This transformation took place in 2004 and was the first such ecumenical partnership between the three largest international Christian mission societies. Today the turnaround of ships is very fast and the seafarer does not usually need accommodation, so the upkeep of duplicate facilities is eliminated and resources can be concentrated on providing modern means of communication through the Internet, money exchange and transfer, and a minibus linking all parts of the port, including the oil terminal at Fawley.

## THE ROYAL NAVAL RESERVE

The Royal Naval Volunteer Reserve was created early in the twentieth century to enable those with no seafaring background to train to fulfil roles in the Royal Navy in times of national emergency. It therefore followed the pattern of the Royal Naval Reserve, which was open only to merchant seafarers and fishermen.

The formation of shore-based divisions, of which there would eventually be twelve, began in 1939. However the Solent Division, known as HMS *Wessex*, did not become established in Southampton until 1947. The first headquarters ship was HMS *Derg*, based in the south-west corner of Inner Dock at 14 Berth. She was renamed HMS *Wessex* in June 1951, but did not last long and was replaced by the Black Swan class frigate HMS *Erne* on 9 April 1952. This ship was commissioned as HMS *Wessex* in June of that year at the same time as a women's unit was formed. In 1954 a Thornycroft-built minesweeper, HMS *Warsash*, formerly HMS *Alfriston*, was acquired for seagoing training.

As the Royal Naval Volunteer Reserve and the Royal Naval Reserve were combined in 1958, Wessex became part of the RNR. When the Inner Dock closed in February 1963, HMS *Wessex* was the last ship out and went to Ocean Dock. A shore-based HMS *Wessex* was established in the former Marine Airport Terminal building at 50 Berth and the commissioning ceremony was performed by Admiral of the Fleet, Earl Mountbatten of Burma, on 30 August 1963. The new station made the old headquarters ship HMS *Wessex* redundant and it was towed away for disposal. A coastal minesweeper, HMS *Solent*, and an inshore minesweeper, HMS *Isis*, were available for training in the early 1970s, although HMS *Isis* had been discarded by 1974. *Wessex* closed in 1994.

## AIRPORT

Aviation may seem a curious partner for a port, but pioneers of aviation and high-speed craft such as Noel Pemberton-Billing, Hubert Scott-Paine and Reginald Mitchell were all based locally. Their developments in the field of aviation, whether of seaplanes or flying boats, went on to gain these men international recognition for their work.

Even in the early twentieth century the desire for rapid transport links was being expressed. As a consequence, a pioneering but short-lived passenger flying boat service was established in Southampton just after the First World War. The next such venture was started in 1923 by the British Marine Air Navigation Co. Ltd, with routes from Southampton to the Channel Islands, Cherbourg and Le Havre.

In 1934, the government established the Empire Mail Service, mirroring what had been done in shipping nearly a century before. Flying boats were ideal for these bulk cargoes and a small number of passengers could also be carried in relative luxury. Imperial Airways began operating from Southampton in February 1937. The actual point of departure within the Docks moved, as passengers on the earlier flights were transferred by launch from the Docks to the company depot in Hythe. Later, 101 Berth was used and then 109 Berth, where a terminal building was constructed. During the Second World War flying boat services were transferred to Poole, although the terminal building remained and became a base for the US Army Transportation Corps.

The location of the Empire Air Base was a matter of debate. Southampton Harbour Board naturally wanted it to be within its sphere of influence and discussed various schemes with the Air Ministry, which favoured a permanent base at Langstone Harbour, near Portsmouth. The debate rumbled on during the Second World War and plans were published in January 1944 for a marine air base at the junction of the Solent and Southampton Water. Then, in July 1946, the Harbour Board announced the return to Southampton of Imperial Airways, now trading as BOAC. This time the terminal would be at 50 Berth and the *Echo* reported that this 'temporary base would be in operation next summer', although in the event operations didn't begin until 31 March 1948. The revival was indeed temporary as BOAC ceased operating from the base in October 1950 and the Marine Air Terminal closed with the arrival of the last inward flight from Marseilles by the flying boat *Somerset* on 14 November.

Despite this setback it was still hoped that Southampton could once again be Britain's principal marine air base. The Saunders Roe 'Princess' which finally took to the air in 1953 seemed at first to be a suitable aircraft, but no engines of sufficient power were available at the time to make it a commercial success. At the same time, economical, rapid air travel from land-based 'airports' was becoming the preferred mode of travel for an increasing number of passengers.

There was a brief reprieve for Southampton-based air services. Aquila Airways Ltd, a private flying boat operator, had been formed in 1948 using two former BOAC craft. Initially the firm was involved in the Berlin Airlift, but began to offer a service from Southampton to Madeira in May 1949, making the very first commercial flight to the island.

Aquila made other achievements of note. The company made the first flight from Britain to the Falkland Islands in June 1952, and on 9 August that year undertook a series of experimental flights for the Air Ministry, taking servicemen and their families to Singapore. All troops bound for overseas had, until then, embarked from Southampton, which had become the trooping port of the country. The flight to the Far East took six days compared with the twenty-eight-day sea voyage, and led directly to the change from ship to air as a means of moving the armed forces over long distances.

Aquila could continue operating only because the Harbour Board, still keen to promote aviation, had become licensees for the Marine Airport after BOAC left and had restored the facilities, including radio communication with air traffic control centres. Initially the prospects seemed good; a proving flight to Glasgow was held on 1 June 1950, and the company applied to the Air Ministry in October 1953 to start a service to Capri. New services were started to Las Palmas in 1956 and to Montreux in Switzerland in 1957, but rising costs and the difficulty of securing replacement aircraft meant that the company finally ceased trading in September 1958. There may have been other factors affecting the demise of flying boats. A senior BOAC pilot told the author many years ago that flotsam was a regular cause of damage to his machine.

Back in the period between the two World Wars, the Southern Railway, which owned the Docks, was a partner with Imperial Airways and with the other three railway companies of the day in establishing Railway Air Services Ltd in March 1934. The first flights were from Croydon, not Southampton, but Southampton (Eastleigh) soon became part of this pioneering network of internal and mainly seasonal services. There were limited wartime operations which did not include Southampton and although Railway Air Services was a successful company, it ceased operating in January 1947. Its routes were taken over by British European Airways, then the national operator.

Southampton made another significant contribution to the history of aviation when Twyford Moors Helicopters Ltd obtained the backing of the City Council in 1968 to develop a 15 acre (6 hectare) plot of land to the west of the Skyway Hotel and between West Quay Road and the Western Docks. Southampton Heliport was the first such facility in any British city and was officially opened by Earl Mountbatten of Burma on 24 May 1969. The owner's intention was to use it as a base for private charter work and also to undertake survey operations of the electricity grid and in connection with oil and gas pipelines. Unfortunately there seems not to have been sufficient interest and the facility closed in about 1974. (The 125-room independent Skyway Hotel, with its main entrance in Herbert Walker Avenue, opened in July 1966. It is now the Holiday Inn.)


## THE FUTURE

Over the centuries Southampton has had periods of prosperity and of relative decline in its trade. Associated British Ports has a new plan on which it is consulting a wide spectrum of interested parties and the outcome of which will indicate the best way forward. Development is not a reaction to external forces, but comes out of a knowledge and understanding of the industry and likely trends, and making provision for events that are on the horizon.

Longer term prediction is more uncertain. Perhaps the only certainty is that people will not be correct in their vision of the future. In 1977 the British Transport Docks Board took part in an experiment. Delegates attending an international conference in Houston were asked to make predictions for their ports' performance, to be included in a time capsule to be opened in 2014, the centenary of the Port of Houston. The vision for Southampton was that it would be an off-shore super port acting as a trans-shipment locus for Northern Europe, thereby reducing the need for sixth-generation, 150,000 ton container ships which would otherwise clog up the Channel. There would be a three-hour working day and, as part of the leisure industry, there would be civilian aircraft carriers taking people's private aircraft across the Atlantic. While utopian in many ways, this was a fuel-hungry future and although it was realised that oil reserves in the North Sea would eventually run out, a return to coal imported in fluidised form through Southampton was viewed as the feed-stock for our chemical industry, with some reliance being placed on solar power.

In order that they might speak with one voice where members' collective interests are at stake, despite individually being in competition with each other, the UK Major Ports Group was formed in early 1993 to represent the interests of the industry to the government and the EU. ABP was one of the original seven members. These ports have no government subsidy and therefore depend on the soundness of their business acumen to succeed, so therefore a balance has to be struck between additional duties that might stem from Europe versus commercial return. For similar reasons, the UK Major Ports Group is a member of the European Sea Ports Organisation (ESPO), formed to represent all ports in their dealings with the EU.

In November 2009 the government published a 'Draft National Policy Statement' for Ports, the first for several years. The draft statement emphasised the importance of ports to the national economy and that judgements about development are best made on the basis of commercial factors by ports operating within a free market environment. The conclusion was that there exists a compelling case for substantial additional port investment over the next twenty to thirty years.

Whatever the outcome, the one enduring characteristic of Southampton was identified in 1950 by the man from Thomas Cook, who should have the last word. He said, 'The fact that this port is the haven of so many fine ships probably instils subconsciously in the people associated with the place an extra touch of pride'.

The George & Vulture public house in Castle Court in the City of London has served its community for centuries and continues to do so today. It has many claims to fame having been a meeting place for the Hellfire Club and a residence of Charles Dickens. It was here that the first general meeting of the Southampton Dock Co. was held on 18 August 1836.

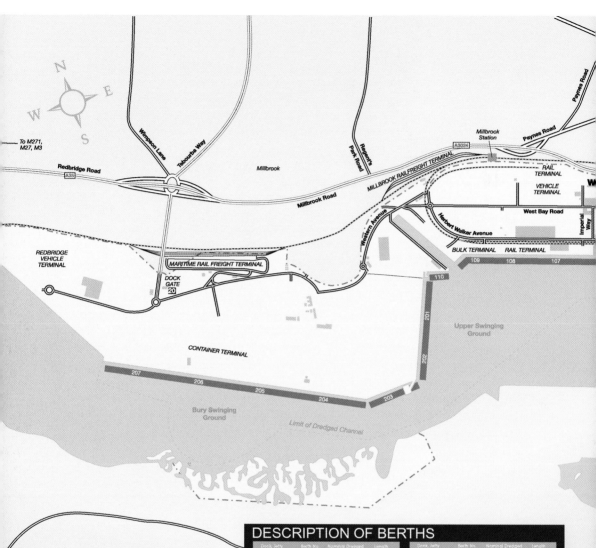

**N W E S**

To M271,
M27, M3

Redbridge Road
A35

Winnson Lane
Tebourba Way

Regent's Park Road

Millbrook

Millbrook Road

MILLBROOK RAILFREIGHT TERMINAL

Western Avenue

Paynes Road

Millbrook
Station
A3024

Paynes Road

RAIL
TERMINAL

VEHICLE
TERMINAL

Herbert Walker Avenue

West Bay Road

Imperial Way

BULK TERMINAL    RAIL TERMINAL
109    106    107

MARITIME RAIL FREIGHT TERMINAL

REDBRIDGE
VEHICLE
TERMINAL

DOCK
GATE
20

110

201

Upper Swinging
Ground

CONTAINER TERMINAL

207    206    205    204    203

202

Bury Swinging
Ground

Limit of Dredged Channel

To Totton,
A35 & M27

Marchwood bypass

# Present extent of the
# Port of Southampton

**ABP**

ABP Southampton
Ocean Gate, Atlantic Way, Southampton SO14 3QN

Tel: +44 (0)23 8048 8800
Fax: +44 (0)23 8033 6402
Email: southampton@abports.co.uk
www.abports.co.uk

Marchwood bypass

## DESCRIPTION OF BERTHS

| Dock, Jetty or Quay | Berth No. | Nominal Dredged Depth at Lowest Low Water (metres) | Length of quays (metres) | Dock, Jetty or Quay | Berth No. | Nominal Dredged Depth at Lowest Low Water (metres) | Length of quays (metres) |
|---|---|---|---|---|---|---|---|
| Berths | 201 | 10.2 | 380 | Ocean Dock | 43-44 | 11.7 | 480 |
| | 202 | 12.2 | 274 | (Entrance 121.9 m wide) | 45 | 10.2 | 190 |
| | 203 | 9.1 | 274 | | 46 | 10.2 | 280 |
| Container Berths | 204 | 13.6 | 310 | | 47 | 11.7 | 260 |
| | 205 | 12.8 | 310 | Test Quays | 48 | 7.1 | 190 |
| | 206 | 13.6 | 310 | | 49 | 7.1 | 120 |
| | 207 | 16.0 | 420 | | 40 | 0.3 | 150 |
| Western Docks | 101-2 | 10.2 | 370 | | 41 | 8.7 | 172 |
| | 102-3 | 10.2 | 310 | | 38-39 | 10.5 | 366 |
| | 103-4 | 10.2 | 340 | Dock Head | 37 | 7.8 | 143 |
| | 105 | 11.7 | 200 | Empress Dock | 30-31 | 7.6 | 286 |
| | 106 | 11.7 | 260 | (Entrance 43.6 m wide) | 32-33 | 6.6 | 308 |
| | 106-7 | 11.7 | 110 | | 24-25 | 7.1 | 198 |
| | 107-109 | 11.2 | 760 | | 26-27 | 7.1 | 240 |
| | 110 | 10.2 | | | 20 | 5.6 | 120 |
| | | | | Itchen Quays | 50-53 | 9.1 | 263 |
| | | | | | 34-36 | 2.5 | 380 |

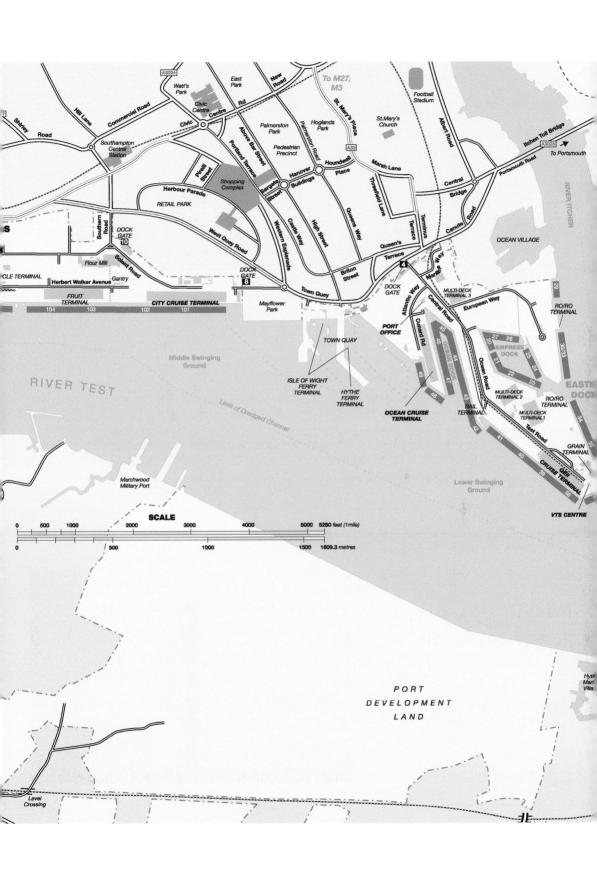

Watt's Park

East Park

New Road

To M27, M3

Football Stadium

Hill Lane

Commercial Road

Civic Centre Rd

St. Mary's Place

St. Mary's Church

Shirley Road

A3024

Civic Centre

Albert Road

Ichen Toll Bridge

A3025

To Portsmouth

Southampton Central Station

Palmerston Park

Hoglands Park

Portland Terrace

Above Bar Street

Palmerston Road

A33

Portsmouth Road

RIVER ITCHEN

Pirelli Street

Pedestrian Precinct

Houndwell Place

Marsh Lane

Central Bridge

OCEAN VILLAGE

Shopping Complex

Hanover Buildings

Bargate Street

Threefield Lane

Terminus Terrace

Canute Road

Harbour Parade

RETAIL PARK

West Quay Road

Western Esplanade

Castle Way

High Street

Queens Way

Queen's Terrace

DOCK GATE 10

Southern Road

Flour Mill

Solent Road

Gantry

Briton Street

DOCK GATE 8

Town Quay

DOCK GATE

Atlantic Way

Central Road

Marsh Way

MULTI-DECK TERMINAL 3

European Way

RO/RO TERMINAL

29

..CLE TERMINAL

Herbert Walker Avenue

FRUIT TERMINAL

CITY CRUISE TERMINAL

104  103  102  101

Mayflower Park

PORT OFFICE

Cunard Rd

45

46

OCEAN DOCK

44

47

Ocean Road

EMPRESS DOCK

27  26

20

21  22

23  24

25

30 33

EASTE.. DOC..

Middle Swinging Ground

TOWN QUAY

49

43

OCEAN CRUISE TERMINAL

RAIL TERMINAL

MULTI-DECK TERMINAL 2

MULTI-DECK TERMINAL1

RO/RO TERMINAL

34

RIVER TEST

ISLE OF WIGHT FERRY TERMINAL

HYTHE FERRY TERMINAL

Limit of Dredged Channel

42

41

Test Road

GRAIN TERMINAL

40

QEII CRUISE TERMINAL

39

Marchwood Military Port

Lower Swinging Ground

38

VTS CENTRE

SCALE

| 0 | 500 | 1000 | 2000 | 3000 | 4000 | 5000 | 5280 feet (1mile) |

| 0 | 500 | 1000 | 1500 | 1609.3 metres |

PORT DEVELOPMENT LAND

Level Crossing

Hyt.. Mari.. Villa..

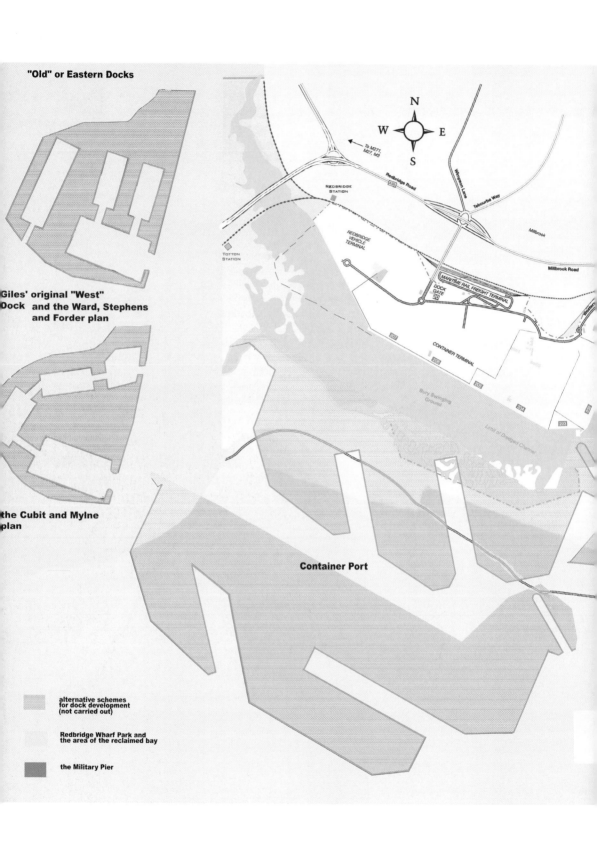

**"Old" or Eastern Docks**

**Giles' original "West" Dock** and the Ward, Stephens and Forder plan

**the Cubit and Mylne plan**

**Container Port**

To M271, M27, M3

Redbridge Road

Wimpson Lane

Tebourba Way

Millbrook

REDBRIDGE STATION

Millbrook Road

REDBRIDGE VEHICLE TERMINAL

TOTTON STATION

MARITIME RAIL FREIGHT TERMINAL

DOCK GATE 20

CONTAINER TERMINAL

Bury Swinging Ground

Limit of Dredged Channel

N
W        E
S

alternative schemes for dock development (not carried out)

Redbridge Wharf Park and the area of the reclaimed bay

the Military Pier

# Waterfront Southampton

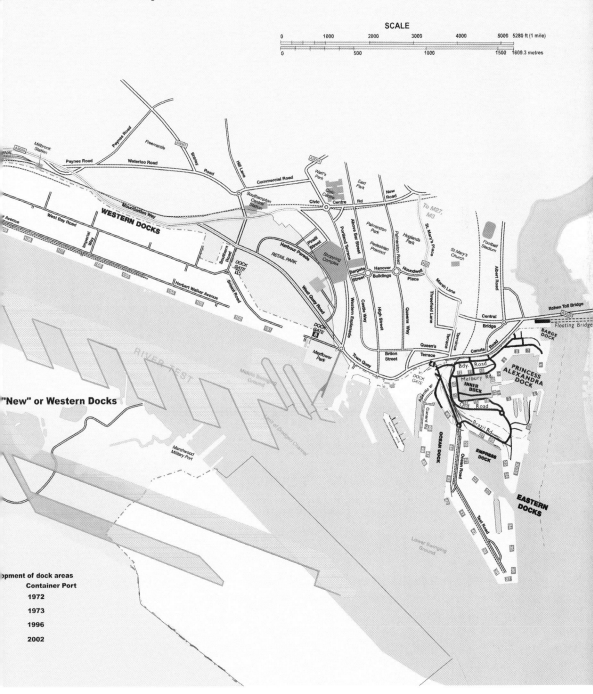

# REFERENCES

## JOURNALS AND PERIODICALS

*Docks,* British Transport Docks board, Current from 1964 (January) to *c.* 1981 – monthly

*Echo*, as referred to in the text.

Extract from the 'Accounts of Southampton Town, 1449 – 1450', from a transcript by Sheila Thomson

*Lock and Quay,* Docks and Inland Waterways Executive, Current from *c.* 1949 to *c.* 1963 – monthly

*Ports,* Associated British Ports, Current 1982 to date – monthly until March 1984; bi-monthly to Winter 1992; then quarterly

*SCT Facts and Figures* (Southampton Container Port, n.d. *c.* 1990)

Southampton 'Cruise Capital of Northern Europe' in *Seatrade Cruise Review,* 2009

*Southampton Docks and Shipping Guide,* Current from 1922 to 1975 – monthly

Southampton Dock Co. minutes

*Southampton Port Handbook,* Current *c.* 1930 to date.

Southampton 'Cruise Capital of Northern Europe' in *Seatrade Cruise Review,* 2009

Supplement to *South Africa* No. 9, 1923

*Transactions of the Institute of Naval Architects,* Vol. XXXVI, 1895.

## BOOKS

Arnott, Alastair, *Maritime Southampton* (Breedon Books, 2002)

Batchelor-Smith, L.A., *Loom of Memories* (BAT Co. Ltd, Millbrook, 1969)

Baynes, H. (?), *Southampton and its Commercial Prospects* (London 1841)

Carr, Laughton, L.G., *The Victoria History of the Counties of England: A History of Hampshire and the Isle of Wight Vol. V: Maritime History* (London, Constable & Company, 1912)

Davies, Revd J.S., *A History of Southampton* (Gilbert & Co., Southampton, 1883)

Dixon, John, *On the Harbour and Docks of Southampton* (Institution of Naval Architects, 1894)

Friel, Ian, *Maritime History of Britain and Ireland* (British Museum, 2003)

Hull, Norman, *Eagles Over Water: The Story of Aquila Airways* (Baron, 1995)

Knowles, Bernard, *Southampton: The English Gateway* (Hutchinson & Co., 1951)

Levinson, Marc, *The Box: How the Shipping Container made the World Smaller and the World Economy Bigger* (Princeton University Press, 2008).

Mann, John Edgar, *Southampton Past and Present* (Countryside Books, Newbury, 1985).

Monkhouse, F.J. (Ed.), *A Survey of Southampton and Its Region* (British Association for the Advancement of Science, 1964)

Mudie, Robert, *Hampshire: Its Past and Present Condition and Future Prospects Vol. 1* (Winchester, n.d. *c.* 1839)

Patterson, A. Temple, *A History of Southampton Vol. III 1700-1914* (Southampton University Press, 1975)

Platt, Colin, *Medieval Southampton: The Port and Trading Community, AD 1000-1600* (Routledge & Kegan Paul, London, 1973).

Rendel Esq., A.M., 'Southampton Harbour Report' (1884)

Shillington, E.A., *The Story of Southampton Harbour* (G.F. Wilson, 1947)

Southampton Dock Co., *The Port of Southampton* (self-published, 1882)

Southern Railway, *A Souvenir of Southampton Docks* (Southern Railway, n.d. *c.* 1930, reprinted by Southampton University Industrial Archaeology Group, 1982)

Stephens, E.L., 1. Commercial Docks on the South Coast of England (Southampton, 22 December, 1835)

Stephens, E.L., 2. Commercial Docks at Southampton (August, 1837)

Taylor, Miles (Ed.), *Southampton: Gateway to the British Empire* (I.B Tauris & Co. Ltd, 2007).

Ticehurst, Brian J., Southampton Seaman's Home, Oxford Street: RMS Titanic Connections (Southampton City Council, 2006)

The Report of Messrs Cubitt and Mylne to the Southampton Dock Co. at its offices at 26 Austin Friars, London, on 1 March 1839.

*Thornycroft Activities* (J.I. Thornycroft, 1930)

Turner, J.M.W., Collins, W., Westall, W., Prout, S., Dewint, P., and others, *An Antiquarian and Picturesque Tour round the Southern Coast of England* (Nattali, London, 1849)

Womack J., Jones, D., and Roos, D., *The Machine that Changed the World* (Simon & Schuster, 1990)

# INDEX

Visit our website and discover thousands of other History Press books.

## www.thehistorypress.co.uk